NEW Proficiency Writing

Mary Stephens

CONTENTS MAP

1 Writing to the Editor

1 Read the question

Read the exam question below carefully.

Part 1

You **must** answer this question. Write your answer in **300–350 words** in an appropriate style.

The extract below is part of a newspaper article on environmental matters which you read recently. The editor invited readers to comment on the article. You have decided to write a letter to the paper, responding to the points raised and giving your own views.

> We all worry about global warming. The problem, however, is that there is very little we can do about it without returning to the 'dark ages'. The fact is, the very things that cause global warming are now essential to our lives. We need the energy from power stations to drive our industries. We can't do without our cars, for example, or our refrigerators, or our mobile phones, or the millions of other goods we use and throw away each year. In the face of all this, is there really anything we can do to tackle the problem?

Write your **letter**. Do not write any postal addresses.

exam information

In Part 1 of the Writing Paper, you will be given some input material, usually in the form of one or two texts. You need to read the instructions (rubric) *and* the text(s) carefully and use *both* as the basis for your writing. You may have to write a letter, an article, an essay or a proposal. All these text types will have a discursive function in Part 1. In other words, you will have to present and develop arguments, express and support opinions, evaluate ideas, etc.

exam tip

In Part 1 of the exam you will lose marks if you do not cover all the points you are asked for. It is extremely important that you read the rubrics and the input material very carefully.

2 Think about your reader

Work with a partner. Look at the instructions (rubric) in the exam question again and answer the following questions.

1 What kind of publication does the extract come from?

2 Who has invited you to write a letter?

3 Who is going to read your letter, besides the person who has invited you to write?

exam tip

In the exam, the letters you may be required to write will probably be formal or semi-formal.

3 Think about register

a Read the letter below which another reader wrote to the same newspaper on a different topic.

Dear Sir or Madam,

I am writing to you about the article on out-of-town shopping centres, which you published last week. The article raised a number of issues, which I would like to comment on here.

In the article, the writer claims that out-of-town centres are to be commended because they provide a range of shops under one roof, so the centres are 'convenient and accessible'. I am afraid I have to disagree. Not being a motorist myself, I find these centres anything but convenient.

Furthermore, I would like to remind you of the environmental consequences of building shopping outlets outside towns. Large areas of the countryside are inevitably swallowed up for development, more roads are built, and pollution is increased due to the fact that motorists use their cars to drive to these centres.

Surely it would be better to keep shopping centres in the centre of our towns and cities. In that way, we could limit the impact on the countryside while at the same time making the centres accessible to all, not just the motorist.

Yours faithfully,

Sandra West

b Now study the list below. It includes some of the characteristics of formal language. Find examples of these in the letter in **a**.

- complex sentences
- sophisticated vocabulary used with precision
- passive forms
- polite or diplomatic phrasing
- participle clauses
- relative clauses

c Should *your* letter be formal or informal?

4 Identify the key points in the question

a Work with a partner. Look at the instructions (rubric) in the exam question again and answer the following question.

Why have you decided to write a letter? To comment on what the writer says in the article? To give your own opinions? For some other reason?

b Now look at the extract in the exam question again and answer the following questions.

1. How does the writer suggest we all feel about global warming?
2. What does he/she think we can do about the problem?
3. What examples does he/she give of things that cause global warming?
4. Why is it so difficult to tackle the problem, according to the writer?
5. What question does the writer ask at the end of his/her article?

exam tip

It is a good idea to underline the key points you need to address in the exam question. In that way, you will be sure you don't leave anything out.

Factfile

Cars, factories and power stations all emit poisonous gases, including carbon dioxide, into the atmosphere; these add to air pollution. The increase in carbon dioxide in the Earth's atmosphere causes the gradual warming of the Earth, which is called global warming. As a result of global warming, we are witnessing climate change. We can reduce pollution levels by using less energy and cutting gas emissions. We could cut down on manufacturing in factories if we demanded fewer consumer goods like refrigerators and washing machines. We can develop cleaner technologies by producing cleaner petrol, for example. Cars cause pollution and congestion. Other ways of travelling are less harmful to the environment.

5 Brainstorm the topic

Work with a partner and answer the questions. Note down the best ideas.

1 Why do we need power stations? And factories?
2 In what ways do factories and power stations pollute our environment? Is there any way we can control this other than shutting them down completely?
3 Do you think people need all the consumer goods they buy at present? Do you think they throw them away too quickly?
4 How do cars damage the environment? Is there any way we can reduce the damage other than banning them?
5 In your opinion, can we and should we tackle the problem of global warming? How?

6 Make a plan

Work with a partner and answer the questions.

a Look at the following notes which one student has made. Tick (✔) the points you think she should include in the letter. Put a cross (✗) against any points that are irrelevant or unimportant.

- reason for writing: to comment on the article
- why I disagree with the writer about what we can do
- why we should and must tackle the problem
- habitat destruction
- how we can reduce emissions from power stations
- why we should use fewer consumer goods
- other ways to reduce global warming e.g. using cleaner technologies
- world poverty
- conclusion/summary of my views

tip

It is essential to plan what you are going to write *before you start.* Otherwise, your writing will be confused and difficult for the reader to follow.

b Look at the plan below. The student has already completed the plan for the first and last paragraph of her letter. Decide which points she should put in each of the remaining paragraphs.

Paragraph 1: Reason for writing: to comment on the article

Paragraph 2: ....

Paragraph 3: ....

Paragraph 4: ....

Paragraph 5: Conclusion/summary of my views

tip

A formal or semi-formal letter usually begins by stating briefly the reason for writing.

7 Think about style

When writing to an editor or a person in a position of authority, you need to adopt a tone that is not too direct or aggressive. Look at the pairs of phrases below and tick (✔) the ones that are more tentative or diplomatic.

1 **a** You say that …
b You appear to claim that …

2 **a** I'm afraid I disagree.
b You are wrong.

3 **a** You must not say that.
b I think it is dangerous to say that.

4 **a** I would like to suggest that you should …
b Why don't you …?

5 **a** I expect you to …
b I would be grateful if you would …

8 Read a model letter

Read the model letter below and answer the following questions.

Has the writer:

1 covered all the points in the exam question?
2 used an appropriate format and style?
3 stated her reason for writing?
4 produced well-reasoned arguments?
5 stated her opinion clearly?
6 linked sentences and paragraphs together appropriately?
7 included any irrelevant points?
8 rounded off her letter in a suitable way?

56 Sunderbury Road
West Heath
Yorkshire YH3 4HD
3rd March 200-

The Editor
The Daily News
Lime Street
Yorkshire YM9

Dear Sir/Madam,

I am writing to you about the article on global warming which appeared in your newspaper last Saturday. It raised some basic issues which I feel very strongly about and I think all your readers need to consider them carefully.

At the start of the article, the writer appears to claim that the situation with regard to global warming is hopeless. I am afraid I disagree. What is more, I think that if we fail to take action now, the consequences for our planet will be disastrous.

In my opinion, we have to work together to persuade industry to cut emissions of gases from factories and power stations. However, this does not mean that we have to return to the 'dark ages'. It is possible to reduce the number of goods we manufacture without cutting production completely. On the other hand, I do feel the consumer society has gone too far. In our 'throw away' society, things cost more to repair than to replace. This is all wrong. We need to make things that last. If we did this, it would automatically lead to a reduction in manufacturing.

There are other ways we can tackle global warming, too. Industries could be persuaded to develop cleaner technologies. This has already begun in the car industry, where they are developing vehicles that do not burn petrol. Of course, public transport should be encouraged too, as it is a better alternative to the private car and causes less pollution.

In conclusion, I want to say that it is dangerous to suggest that all our efforts to tackle global warming are useless. We can and must do something about it. And moreover, we can do this without destroying our economy or altering our lifestyles completely.

Yours faithfully,

Jessica Burton
Jessica Burton

9 Think about paragraphing

a Summarise the topic of each of the paragraphs in the model text in the template below.

Paragraph 1: Reason for writing: to comment on the article

Paragraph 2: ....

Paragraph 3: ....

Paragraph 4: ....

Paragraph 5: Concluding remarks/summary: It is dangerous to say we can do nothing because we *can* make a difference without crippling our economies/altering our lifestyles completely.

tip

Paragraphs act as stepping stones in a text and make it easier for the reader to follow. You should start a new paragraph each time you introduce a new topic in your writing.

b Do each of the paragraphs in the model letter contain a topic sentence? Find them and underline them.

tip

Most paragraphs contain a **topic sentence**. A topic sentence should summarise the theme of the paragraph. The other sentences in the paragraph explain, exemplify or expand the information in the topic sentence.

c Did the writer use paragraphs in her letter in the same way as you suggested in **6b**?

10 Think about language

a Underline the words the writer uses in the model letter to show addition and contrast.

b Put each of the linking words and phrases into the appropriate column.

furthermore	although
on the other hand	moreover
what's more	however
nevertheless	added to this

Contrast	Addition
....	....
....	....
....	....
....	....

c Which phrase does the writer use to introduce her concluding paragraph? Which of the phrases below could you use instead?

All in all, ...	At the end, ...
To sum up, ...	At last, ...

11 Think about vocabulary

Collocations

a Match the verbs (1–6) that collocate with the nouns (a–f).

1	make	**a**	a problem
2	solve	**b**	steps/action
3	cut	**c**	a suggestion/a point
4	protect/conserve	**d**	an issue/an objection
5	raise	**e**	emissions/production
6	take	**f**	the environment

b Underline the correct option.

1 I feel very *hardly / strongly* about these matters.
2 In your article, you *refuse / claim* there is nothing more we can do.
3 We need to take immediate *measures / measurements* to reduce pollution.
4 The steps I have suggested would *guide / lead* to a reduction in pollution.
5 If we *fail / neglect* to act soon, the consequences could be disastrous.
6 I do not agree that what we are doing is a *loss / waste* of time.

12 Exam practice: Write a letter to the editor

You are going to write a letter to an editor. Read the exam question and follow the instructions below.

Part 1

You **must** answer this question. Write your answer in **300–350 words** in an appropriate style.

The extract below is part of a newspaper article on culture and traditions. Readers were asked to send in their opinions. You have decided to write a letter responding to the points raised and expressing your own views.

> We are losing our individual customs and traditions. In these days of cheap, fast air travel and modern technology, different countries are becoming more and more alike. Whichever country we come from, we are likely to listen to the same music, to wear the same clothes, and to watch the same films. Young people often know little about the traditions of the area they come from. Should nations try to preserve the customs that make us different from each other and, if so, how can we achieve this?

Write your **letter**. Do not write any postal addresses.

- **Read the question**
  Underline all the points asked for in the exam question (including rubric and input material) and include them in your letter.
- **Brainstorm the topic**
  Note down ideas and make a plan before you begin.
- **Think about format**
  See page 14 for the layout of a formal letter.
- **Think about your reader**
  Write in a style appropriate for a formal letter and use this style consistently. Do not use an aggressive tone.
- **Think about paragraphing**
  Organise your ideas into clear paragraphs around one topic sentence. Begin by giving your reason for writing and referring to the newspaper article.

2 Supporting an issue

1 Read the question

Read the exam question below carefully.

exam information

In Part 1 of the Writing Paper, you may be given visual as well as written input.

Part 1

You **must** answer this question. Write your answer in **300–350 words** in an appropriate style.

The road through the centre of your village is becoming increasingly busy and dangerous. Last night you saw the article below in a local newspaper. You have decided to write to your local council, referring to the accident described in the article and stating your concern about the traffic situation. You should also state your support for the bypass and make a suggestion about what should happen next.

Boy Injured in Accident Blackspot

Local teenager, Tom Smith, 15, had a miraculous escape when he was hit by a lorry outside the gates of his school yesterday. The lorry skidded and crashed after taking the bend at Bailey's Bridge too quickly. It is the third accident in the village this month. 'There is just too much traffic going through our village these days,' complained headmaster Stephen Brown. 'We desperately need a bypass. I've written to the council and even sent them a diagram showing where the bypass could go, but I've had no reply.' He appealed to residents who support his proposal to write to the council urgently.

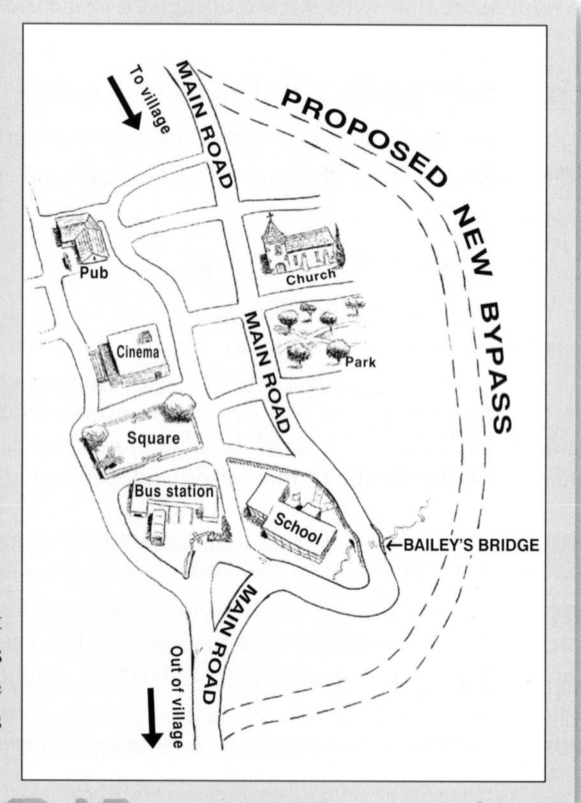

Write your **letter**. Do not write any postal addresses.

2 Think about your reader

Work with a partner. Look at the instructions (rubric) in the exam question again and answer the following questions.

1 Who have you decided to write to?
2 What is their role in the village?
3 Who do they represent?
4 How can they help?
5 As a resident writing on a serious topic, how should you address these people in a letter? Should your tone be formal or informal?

3 Identify the key points in the question

a Work with a partner. Look at the instructions (rubric) in the exam question again and answer the following questions.

1 Where do you live?
2 What's wrong with the road through the village?
3 Where did you see the article about a recent accident?
4 You are asked to do four things in your letter. What are they? Underline them in the exam question.

b Now look at the extract in the exam question again and answer the following questions.

1 What happened yesterday?
2 Where and why did it happen?
3 Is it the first time something like this has happened?
4 What does the headmaster blame? What does he want the council to do?
5 How have the council reacted so far?
6 What does the headmaster urge other residents to do? Why?

c Should *your* letter be formal or informal?

Factfile

The council is the organisation responsible for local government in a particular region in Britain. Members of the council are called councillors. They make decisions on certain local issues like roads, traffic, housing etc.

4 Brainstorm the topic

Work with a partner. Imagine you are residents in the village. Discuss these questions and note down the best ideas.

1. Why is the road through your village getting busier? Where is all the extra traffic coming from/going to?
2. Why is the road unsuitable for the increased level of traffic? Is it too narrow/too steep/too dark? Has it got too many sharp bends/narrow bridges?
3. What reasons could you use to persuade the council to consider building a bypass? What could you claim will happen if something is not done soon?
4. How do you think other residents feel about the situation?
5. What suggestions could you make to the council? Call a public meeting? Conduct a survey? Something else?

5 Think about format

Work with a partner and answer the following questions. Can you remember how to set out a formal letter in English? Indicate where the following items should appear on the template.

- your address
- the date
- your name
- the name and address of the recipient
- the greeting (*Dear X,*)
- closing phrase (*e.g. I look forward to hearing from you.*)
- the ending (*e.g. Yours faithfully,*)

1

2

3

4

....

....

....

....

....

....

....

....

....

5

6

7

tip

In the exam, you are **not** required to write any postal addresses in your letter.

6 Make a plan

Look at the plan below. The student has already completed most of the plan for his letter. What points should he include in paragraph 4? Write them in.

Paragraph 1: Reason for writing – concern about traffic and accidents
Paragraph 2: The fact that level of traffic has risen
Why this has happened
Paragraph 3: Why the village can't cope with this amount of traffic
Paragraph 4: ....

7 Think about register

Now study the list below. Which of the following would you *not* expect to find in a formal letter? Mark them with a cross (✗).

- aggressive language
- a large number of phrasal verbs
- idiomatic language or slang
- passive forms
- a personal tone
- a number of very short sentences
- a number of complex sentences
- a limited range of vocabulary

8 Think about style

Tick (✔) the more formal option in the pairs of phrases below.

1 a I am writing to express my concern about …
b I thought I would drop you a line about …

2 a I would urge you to …
b I want you to …

3 a You have to …
b May I suggest that you should …

4 a I wonder if we could …
b Can we …

5 a You know very well that …
b As you are no doubt aware, …

6 a I understand that …
b Someone has told me that …

9 Read a model letter

Read the model letter below and answer the following questions.

1 Has the writer covered the four points asked for in the examination question?

2 Has he opened and closed the letter correctly?

Dear Sir or Madam,

I am writing to you to express my deep concern about the traffic problems in our village and the recent spate of accidents.

As you are no doubt aware, the level of traffic through our village has increased at an alarming rate over the past few years. The development of the nearby ferry port has meant that more and more heavy lorries thunder along our roads day and night. Added to this, there has been a sharp rise in the number of private cars, with tourists travelling to and from the passenger ferries.

Our village was not built to cope with this volume of traffic. The sharp bends and narrow bridges pose a high risk to drivers, especially in winter when the roads are icy. Drivers regularly ignore the speed limit and recent attempts at reducing traffic have had little effect. Only last night a teenage boy was knocked down at Bailey's Bridge. Luckily he was not seriously injured but what about the next time? Pedestrians take their lives in their hands every time they cross the road, and the very young and the very old are particularly at risk.

I understand that a proposal has been put forward to build a bypass around the village. This new bypass could be sited so that it runs through the old industrial estate, which is no longer viable. This would ensure that environmental damage to the surrounding area is kept to the minimum. I know the majority of the residents of the village are in favour of this proposal and I would strongly urge the council to look into the matter. May I suggest that a public meeting be organised to take place within the next month? This would give residents the opportunity to put their arguments more fully, and would enable us to hear the council's reactions to the proposal. Between us, I am sure we can find a solution to current traffic issues.

I look forward to hearing from you.

Yours faithfully,

Eric Martin

Eric Martin

10 Think about paragraphing

a A well-written paragraph usually contains a *topic sentence*. This sentence introduces or summarises the main idea of the paragraph. Underline the topic sentences in paragraphs 2, 3 and 4 of the model letter.

b The idea that is summarised in the topic sentence is usually explained, illustrated or developed in the rest of that paragraph. Which paragraph in the model does not follow this pattern? Why not?

11 Think about language

Find phrases in the model letter which mean the same as the words in italics.

1. I'm writing to *tell you how worried I am* about the traffic.
2. I'm concerned about *the large number of accidents that have taken place in a short time.*
3. *As you probably know*, traffic has increased in the village.
4. Lorries thunder along our roads *all the time.*
5. There has been *a sudden increase* in the number of private cars.
6. Our village cannot *deal successfully with* the level of traffic.
7. The bends and bridges *present a danger to* drivers.
8. Pedestrians *put their lives in danger* every time they cross the road.
9. I understand *someone has made a proposal.*
10. *I really want* the council to examine the problem.
11. The meeting should *happen* in the next month.
12. Residents will be able to *express their views* on what should be done.

tip

Remember that passive structures are a common feature of formal writing.

12 Think about grammar

a Look at the model letter again and underline all the passive verbs.

b Make the following sentences passive. Begin with the words given.

1 They are holding a public meeting at this very moment.
A public meeting ....

2 Someone has just put forward a new proposal and the council will discuss it after lunch.
A new proposal ....

3 Yesterday a vehicle knocked down a teenager who was on his way to school and injured him.
Yesterday a teenager ....

4 They must punish drivers who break the speed limit more severely in future.
Drivers ....

5 The proposed bypass is long overdue – they should have built it years ago.
The proposed bypass is long overdue – it ....

6 Fortunately, they are going to introduce a one-way system in the village next year.
Fortunately, a one-way system ....

7 They may complete work on the new road in a year from now.
Work ....

8 When we left the council meeting, representatives from the traffic department were still discussing the matter.
When we left the council meeting, the matter ....

9 They delayed us, so by the time we arrived at the council meeting, they had already taken a vote.
We ....

10 The councillor promised that they would reconsider our proposal at next month's meeting.
The councillor promised that our proposal ....

13 Exam practice: Write a letter supporting an issue

You are going to write a letter in which you support an issue. Read the exam question and follow the instructions below.

Part 1

You **must** answer this question. Write your answer in **300–350 words** in an appropriate style.

You live in a small town. Yesterday you saw the article below in a newspaper. You have decided to write to the local council, referring to the article and stating your concern about the lack of facilities for young people. You should defend young people from their detractors and suggest the council provide a youth club or other facilities in the area.

Are we doing enough for young people in this town?

Recently, the behaviour of young people around the town has been causing disquiet among residents. There have been reports of 'gangs' of teenagers who gather in the town centre in the evenings, causing a nuisance. 'They block the pavements so pedestrians have to walk in the road,' one resident complained. 'They skateboard and fool about in the main road, too. It's really dangerous. Sooner or later, there'll be an accident.'

However, the teenagers themselves see things in a different light. 'There's nothing for young people to do in this town,' explained Rachel Burton, 16. 'We need somewhere to meet, like a youth club – and some kind of sports facilities. Older people complain about teenagers but they're not prepared to provide what we need. It's just not fair.'

Write your **letter**. Do not write any postal addresses.

- **Read the question**
  Underline all the points asked for in the exam question (including rubric and input material). Make sure you include them in your letter.
- **Brainstorm ideas**
  Note down ideas to include in your letter.
- **Make a plan**
  Always make a paragraph plan before you start to write.
- **Think about format**
  Remember to set out your letter correctly.
- **Think about style**
  Make sure your language is appropriate for your reader.

3 Complaining

1 Read the question

Read the exam question below carefully.

exam information

In Part 2 of the Writing Paper, unlike Part 1, you will *not* be provided with input material to help you, so you can introduce more of your own ideas. You may have to write a letter, an article, an essay, a proposal, a report or a review. In Part 2, you may be asked to persuade, narrate, evaluate, make recommendations, give information, summarise, etc.

Part 2

Write your answer in **300–350 words** in an appropriate style.

You have just returned from a foreign holiday which you booked through a well-known holiday company. Neither the resort nor the hotel that you stayed at came up to your expectations. You have decided to write a letter to the holiday company complaining about aspects of your holiday and outlining the reasons for your dissatisfaction. In your letter, suggest what steps you think the company should take to rectify the problems for holiday makers in the future, and say what kind of compensation you expect.

Write your **letter**. Do not write any postal addresses.

exam tip

Do not write more than the required number of words (300–350). You will lose marks if your letter becomes rambling or irrelevant. You will probably make more errors, too!

2 Think about your reader

Look at the exam question again and answer the following questions.

1 Who is going to read your letter?
- **a** a friend
- **b** a person working in a company
- **c** a colleague

2 How will you begin your letter?
- **a** Dear Mr or Mrs ...,
- **b** To Whom it May Concern,
- **c** Dear Sir or Madam,

3 For what purpose are you writing? Tick one or more of the following:
- **a** to complain
- **b** to give reasons for something
- **c** to apologise
- **d** to make suggestions
- **e** to request something

4 What impressions do you want your reader to have of you?
- **a** that you are friendly and laid back
- **b** that you are polite but assertive
- **c** that you are angry and abrupt

5 What style of writing will your reader expect?
- **a** formal
- **b** informal and friendly

3 Identify the key points in the question

Work with a partner. Look at the exam question again and answer the following questions.

1 Where have you just returned from?

2 Why were you there?

3 Where did you stay?

4 Who organised your travel and accommodation arrangements?

5 What did you think of your stay?

6 What are the *four* main things you must do in your letter?

4 Brainstorm the topic

Work with a partner and answer the questions. Note down the best ideas.

1 Imagine you have just come back from a disappointing foreign holiday. Where did you go?

2 What was wrong with the resort? Was it too small/crowded? Was it noisy/dirty/over-developed? Was it too far away from civilisation? Was there a different sort of problem?

3 What had the holiday company told you about the resort when you booked your holiday there? How was this description different from the truth?

4 What was wrong with the hotel? Was there something wrong with the service/the facilities/the rooms/the food?

5 How had the hotel been described to you when you booked your holiday? How was it different in reality?

6 What action do you think the holiday company should take with regard to a) the resort and b) the hotel, so that future holiday makers do not suffer in the same way as you have?

7 What kind of compensation do you think you should have?

5 Think about register

Tick (✓) the option in the pairs of sentences below which is more appropriate to use in a letter to the holiday company.

1 **a** The description we were given of the resort was not an accurate one.
b Your staff didn't tell the truth about the resort.

2 **a** Our hotel was rubbish.
b Our hotel fell far short of the standard we were expecting.

3 **a** Please sort things out soon.
b I would be grateful for your prompt attention in this matter.

4 **a** I anticipate receiving a substantial refund.
b I demand a refund.

tip

Language that is rude or aggressive is not appropriate for a formal letter of complaint in English. It is quite possible to make a point strongly while remaining polite and formal.

6 Compare two letters

a Imagine you are an examiner. Read the two letters A and B below. Then use these questions to help you to decide which is better. Say which letter, A or B:

1 does *not* cover all the aspects required in the exam question.
2 is written in the correct tone (i.e. firm but polite).
3 is rambling and confusing.
4 contains complex sentences that are well linked together.
5 contains well-developed paragraphs.
6 addresses the recipient correctly.
7 contains a suitable introduction.
8 contains a final paragraph which is clear and assertive, but not aggressive.
9 contains an appropriate closure.
10 contains a number of punctuation mistakes.
11 is the correct length.

Letter A

Dear Manager,

Recently, I booked a holiday with your company and what a waste of money it was! I am very disgusted with you and your staff and I'd like to know what you plan to do about it. The holiday we had was on page 54 of your brochure and we were there from 13–23 July. My parents paid for my friend and me to go on this holiday so that we could enjoy ourselves and have a good time after our exams.

It cost them a lot of money but they didn't mind, they thought we were going to a good place. When we went to the travel agents the man said that the resort was good for young people but when we got there we found it was full of boring grey haired old people, there was nothing to see and do and nowhere for us to go in the evenings so we were really bored. The hotel was no good because there were no disco's just old fashioned singers and entertainers and everything finished by 10.30 in the evening, we just had to go to bed and it was really disappointing.

The travel agent said that we would have a hotel room with a sea view and a balcony but when we got there our room was at the back and the balcony was so small we could only stand we couldn't sit down or sunbathe. And the view from our room was not of the sea, it was of the back of the hotel where they put all the rubbish. It smelt really bad, too.

I expect to get a refund and an apology.

Best wishes,
Sonya Brown

Letter B

Dear Sir or Madam,

I have just returned from a holiday which I booked with your company and I am writing to say how disappointed I am.

When I booked the holiday together with two friends of mine, we made it clear to your representative that we wanted a small beach resort which was lively but not too noisy or over-developed. He recommended the Arosa resort. He assured us that it was a picturesque little harbour town with plenty to see and do and lots of local colour. He also recommended the Atlantico Hotel and showed us a photo in the brochure of a wonderful room with a balcony and sea view. Although the price of the holiday was more than we had anticipated, we were persuaded to book it.

When we arrived at Arosa, we discovered our mistake. All the town has to offer is a disused and unsightly fishing harbour and a small stony beach which, when we were there, was covered in oil. There was a beautiful, sandy beach in the neighbouring resort but that was 10 kilometres away and we had no transport.

Our hotel was equally disappointing. They are building a new road behind the hotel and the noise and dust was indescribable. We were unable to sit on our balcony at all. Some of the other tourists in the hotel had young children and they were afraid to let them go out alone because it was so dangerous. Another problem was the lifts. They broke down nearly every day so everybody, even the very elderly, had to climb up many flights of stairs. When we complained to the manager, he shrugged and replied that it was 'difficult to get hold of technicians at this time of year'.

As you can imagine, I am disgusted with the holiday we were sold. Regarding the resort, may I suggest that your representatives remove it from your list of recommended destinations or at least give holiday makers a more truthful description in future. The same applies to the hotel. I find it impossible to believe that the lifts cannot be properly maintained at the very least. I also think that the hotel should be closed while dangerous building work is going on.

I would very much like to hear your reactions to all this, and I anticipate receiving an apology and substantial refund from your company.

I look forward to hearing from you.

Yours faithfully,

Bruce Hawkins

tip

When you write a formal letter of complaint:

- start your letter with an introductory paragraph that clearly shows your reason for writing.
- divide the body of your letter into clear, well-linked paragraphs.
- make sure you say what action you expect to be taken about your complaint, for example an apology, a refund, compensation.

b Complete this plan for **Letter B** by writing one phrase or sentence summarising the content of each paragraph.

Paragraph 1: Reason for writing

Paragraph 2: What we were told when we booked

Paragraph 3: ....

Paragraph 4: ....

Paragraph 5: ....

Paragraph 6: Request for compensation

Closing phrase: I look forward to hearing from you.

7 Think about vocabulary

Find words or phrases in **Letter B** which mean the same as the words below.

1 to reserve ....

2 spoilt because it has too many new buildings ....

3 to suggest/advise ....

4 to tell someone something, firmly and with confidence, with the aim of removing doubt ....

5 charming and interesting ....

6 to expect ....

7 no longer in use ....

8 unpleasant to look at ....

9 impossible to describe ....

10 to obtain/find ....

8 Think about paragraphing

Answer the following questions about **Letter B**.

1 Look at Paragraph 1. Is this a good way to start the letter? Why? What does the writer say in this paragraph?

2 What is the main topic of Paragraphs 3, 4 and 5? Underline the topic sentences in each of these paragraphs.

3 Paragraph 6 rounds off the letter in an appropriate way. What does the writer say in this paragraph? Why do you think this is important?

9 Think about punctuation

Read the **Punctuation rules** below. Then look at **Letter A**, Paragraph 2 and find the punctuation mistakes.

Punctuation rules

Apostrophe

You use an apostrophe ('):

- to indicate possession, e.g. *the boy's room* (singular noun + apostrophe = there is one boy); *the boys' room* (plural noun + apostrophe = there are two or more boys)
- to show where letters have been omitted, e.g. *It's a luxurious hotel.*
- for certain shops and businesses. e.g. *the travel agent's.*

Full stop

A full stop (.) marks the end of a sentence. You should begin the next sentence with a capital letter.

Hyphen

You use a hyphen (-) to join the two parts of a compound adjective, e.g. *It was a first-class hotel.*

Comma

You use a comma (,) to divide up a complex sentence so that it is easier to follow:

- to separate items in a list, e.g. *We were looking for a lively resort, a comfortable hotel and picturesque surroundings.*
- to separate a connectors from the rest of the sentence, e.g. *Our hotel, however, was nothing like the one described in the brochure.*
- when you start a sentence with a subordinate clause, e.g. *When we got there, we discovered our mistake.*
- to separate a non-defining relative clause from the main clause, e.g. *Our hotel, which was in the middle of the town, was very noisy.*
- when you start a sentence with a participle clause, e.g. *Looking from the balcony, all we could see was debris.*

10 Exam practice: Write a letter of complaint

You are going to write a letter of complaint. Read the exam question and follow the instructions below.

Part 2

Write your answer in **300–350 words** in an appropriate style.

You have just spent three weeks studying English at a summer school. During your stay, you were provided with accommodation in a large house near the school. Neither the school nor your accommodation came up to your expectations. You have decided to write a letter to the headmaster, explaining the reasons for your dissatisfaction. In your letter, suggest some improvements the headmaster could make and say how you think you should be compensated.

Write your **letter**. Do not write any postal addresses.

- **Read the question**
  Underline all the points asked for in the exam question.
- **Brainstorm the topic**
  Note down some ideas before you start to write.
- **Think about your reader**
  Make sure you use the correct tone and style.
- **Think about paragraphing**
  Use a separate paragraph to start a new topic. Try and include a topic sentence in each paragraph.
- **Edit your letter**
  Always leave time to check spelling, grammar and punctuation.

4 Writing a personal recommendation

1 Read the question

Read the exam question below carefully.

Part 1

You **must** answer this question. Write your answer in **300–350 words** in an appropriate style.

Someone you know has seen the following advertisement in a newspaper.

Would you like to work as a volunteer for an international aid organisation?

Are you:

- aged between 18 and 26?
- a school leaver or an employee looking for a fresh challenge?
- committed to helping others?
- adventurous?
- physically fit?
- resourceful?
- practical?
- able to cope in a crisis?
- able to work as part of a team?
- willing to endure harsh living conditions?

'One World' is an international aid organisation which is looking for volunteers to work on various projects in less privileged parts of the world. Training will be given. No specific professional qualifications are needed.

A young person you know is applying to become a volunteer with this organisation. You think he or she would be very suitable and agree to write a letter of recommendation.

Write your **letter**. Do not write any postal addresses.

2 Think about your reader

Work with a partner. Look at the instructions (rubric) in the exam question again and answer the following questions.

1 Who is going to read your letter?

- **a** an acquaintance
- **b** a stranger
- **c** a friend

2 For what purpose are you writing? Tick (✓) one or more of the following:

- **a** to find out more about the organisation
- **b** to volunteer to work for the organisation
- **c** to give a character reference

3 Think about register

a Read the extract below, which is from a letter a teacher wrote for her student, recommending her for a place at college. Is the letter formal or informal?

> Dear Sir or Madam,
>
> I am writing to you on behalf of Jane Brown, who has been a pupil at this school for the past three years.
>
> Jane is an academically gifted young lady and has consistently come top of her class in examinations. She is especially talented in the arts and has just been awarded one of the country's top scholarships for Music and Drama.
>
> During her time at this school, Jane has shown herself to be a happy, resilient individual, who is popular with her fellow students and teaching staff alike.

b Now study the list below. It includes some of the characteristics features of this type of text. Find examples in the letter in **a**.

- adjectives that describe personal qualities
- present tenses
- relative clauses
- complex sentences
- a range of linking words

c Look at the exam question again. Should *your* letter be formal or informal?

4 Identify the key points in the question

Work with a partner. Look at the instructions (rubrics) and the extract in the exam question again.

1 Who placed the advertisement in the newspaper?
2 What do you know about them?
3 Why did they place the advertisement?
4 Prospective volunteers must meet the requirements listed in the advertisement. How many requirements are there?
5 Where will volunteers work?
6 What sort of professional qualifications do they need, if any?
7 Who has seen the advertisement?
8 What does he or she want you to do?
9 Do you think he or she would make a suitable volunteer?
10 Will the organisation expect:
  a to hear about the applicant's less admirable qualities as well as the good ones?
  b to be given a physical description of the applicant?
  c to be given your reasons why you think the applicant meets all the requirements listed in the advertisement?
  d to be given a list of all the things the applicant has done in his or her life?

5 Brainstorm the topic

Work with a partner. Discuss these questions and note down the best ideas.

1 Imagine the person you are recommending as a volunteer. What is your relationship with this person? How long have you known him or her?

2 Look back at the list of requirements in the advertisement. The advertisement is addressed to potential applicants. Are there any points in the list of requirements that you need not refer to in your recommendation? For example, do you think you need to mention the person's age? Cross out any points you don't need to mention.

3 The person you are recommending has to fit the description in the advertisement. What evidence can you give of this? Note down things the person has done which demonstrate that he or she possesses each of the qualities demanded.
e.g. *He trains and plays football every week with the local team, so he is definitely physically fit. He also goes to the gym every day.*

6 Make a plan

a Which of the requirements in the advertisement are related or linked and can therefore probably be dealt with in the same paragraph?

b Look at the notes one person made below. Have you grouped your notes in the same way she has?

Paragraph 1
Reason for writing: to recommend Jason as a volunteer.

Paragraph 2
I have known Jason for ... years
- Jason is committed to helping others (works as a volunteer in a youth centre).
- He is resourceful/able to cope in a crisis and can deal well with aggressive people/difficult situations in youth centre.

Paragraph 3
- Jason is able to work as part of a team (works closely with other volunteers in the youth centre etc.).

Paragraph 4
- Jason is physically fit (plays football, goes mountaineering etc.)
- He is adventurous/able to endure harsh conditions (goes mountaineering in all sorts of weather, etc).

Paragraph 5
- Jason is practical (has put up shelves, done carpentry round youth centre)

Final paragraph
Summary of reasons why Jason is a suitable candidate.

tip

Remember that you need to justify your statements about the candidate by giving concrete examples to demonstrate his or her personal qualities.

tip

Remember to develop one central idea in a paragraph by writing a topic sentence and then giving examples, illustrations or explanations.

7 Think about vocabulary

a All of the adjectives below describe personal qualities but three of them have a negative meaning. Underline them and give the positive form.

adventurous co-operative inflexible generous helpful level-headed immature reliable resourceful self-motivated sensitive sociable thoughtful tolerant tough selfish

b Rewrite the sentences below replacing the words in italics with a suitable adjective from **a**.

1 Jason is *willing to give money and time to help others* and has done a lot of work for various charities.

2 He is very *good at finding ways of dealing with problems*, so he can cope with almost any circumstances.

3 Having worked for a time as a volunteer firefighter, Jason is *physically resilient and able to cope with difficult or rough conditions.*

4 Jason appears detached but in fact, he is *able to understand and sympathise with other people's feelings and problems.*

5 He is *able to do the things he should do without orders from others*, so he can be left to work without supervision.

6 He is extremely *sensible, down-to-earth and practical*, so he doesn't behave foolishly.

7 He is *trustworthy and dependable*, so you can be sure he will never let you down.

8 Jason is *willing to respect people whose beliefs and backgrounds are different from his own* and gets on well with everybody.

8 Read a model letter

a Read the model letter below and answer the following questions.

Has the writer:

1 covered all the points in the exam question?

2 used the correct style and format?

3 paragraphed her letter correctly?

tip

General recommendations or job references, which are intended for many different employers or interested parties, often start with 'To Whom it May Concern'. However, when the letter of recommendation is for one specific recipient, it may begin in the normal way, with *Dear Sir or Madam*.

4 Writing a personal recommendation

Dear Sir or Madam,

I am writing to you on behalf of Jason Peters, who is applying to work for your organisation.

I have known Jason for four years. We met when he came to work with me as a volunteer at the local youth centre. The centre is in a deprived inner city district and caters for teenagers from difficult backgrounds who are often disturbed or aggressive. Our workers have to be tough and resourceful to cope with the problems they meet, and Jason fits the bill perfectly. He is level-headed and sensible, and his calm, down-to-earth approach to life is a great example to the young people he works with.

One of the most important requirements for us at the youth centre is that we work together as a team. We need to be able to help each other, to listen, and to share our experiences and expertise. Jason does all of these. He is sensitive to the needs of others and extremely tolerant, with the result that he is popular both with his fellow workers and with the young people he is dealing with.

Physically, Jason is very fit. He is a keen sportsman and includes football, baseball and swimming in his list of favourite sports. He regularly plays for the club football team and trains at least three times a week. One of Jason's hobbies is mountaineering and he spends weekends and holidays climbing in the mountains. He is not afraid of physical hardship and has often faced difficult weather and hazardous conditions without complaint. His keen spirit of adventure means that he is keen to take on challenges that other people might shrink from.

Although he has no professional qualifications, Jason has many practical skills. He is good at repairing cars and machinery, and at carpentry – he has put up shelves and made various bits of furniture for our club.

Jason is a generous, thoughtful and resourceful young man and would seem to fit your requirements perfectly. I have no hesitation in recommending him as a volunteer.

Yours faithfully,

Sheena Edwards

b Write a brief summary of each paragraph in the spaces below.

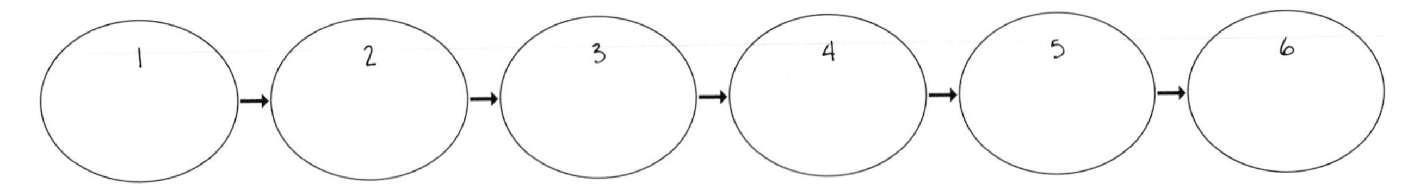

c Is there a topic sentence in each paragraph of the model letter? Underline all the topic sentences you can find.

9 Exam practice: Write a letter of recommendation

You are going to write a letter of recommendation. Read the exam question and follow the instructions below.

Part 1

You **must** answer this question. Write your answer in **300–350 words** in an appropriate style.

You have read the following advertisement in a magazine.

Propose a volunteer

We are proposing to make a TV series about survival. We are looking for eight volunteers who will spend three months together on a remote island.
Volunteers must:

- be aged between 18 and 30
- have a spirit of adventure
- be resilient
- be willing to co-operate with others in a group
- be physically fit
- be resourceful
- be able to cope with a primitive lifestyle
- have a range of practical skills

You know someone who would like to be a volunteer and who you think would be entirely suitable. You decide to write to the magazine, recommending this person.

Write your **letter**. Do not write any postal addresses.

- **Identify the key points in the question**
  Underline the points you have to cover in the exam question and make sure you don't forget any in your answer.
- **Make a plan**
  Group related points together according to topic and make a paragraph plan.
- **Think about vocabulary**
  Use some of the vocabulary you have seen in this unit to describe personal qualities.
- **Think about tenses**
  Remember to use the Present Perfect Simple or Present Perfect Continuous to describe recent, unfinished actions. Make sure you use past tenses to describe actions that finished at a definite past time.

5 Giving an opinion

1 Read the question

Read the exam question below carefully.

Part 2

Write your answer in **300–350 words** in an appropriate style.

A national TV programme recently carried out a survey of young people's habits. The results of the survey indicated that young people are spending far more time using computers than reading books. Viewers have been asked to write in to the makers of the programme suggesting why this is happening and giving their views on which of the two activities is preferable and why.

Write your **letter**. Do not write any postal addresses.

exam tip

In the exam, you may be asked to give your opinion on a topic in a letter.

2 Think about your reader

Look at the exam question again and answer the following questions.

1 Who are viewers invited to write to?

2 How well do you know the people you are going to write to?
- **a** very well
- **b** quite well
- **c** not at all

3 How should you begin and finish your letter?
- **a** Dear Programme Makers,
- **b** Dear Sir or Madam,
- **c** To Whom it May Concern,

4 How serious is the topic you are going to write about?

5 Should your letter be formal or informal?

3 Identify the key points in the question

Look at the exam question again and answer the following questions.

1 Who are you?

2 What have you learnt from the TV survey?

3 The recipient(s) of your letter want you to cover *three* main areas in your letter. What are they? Underline them in the exam question, then complete the list below.

You must:

- *suggest why young people are spending far more time using computers than reading books*
- ....
- ....

tip

Remember that formal letters usually start *Dear ...,* If you don't know the name of the person to whom you are writing, begin with *Dear Sir or Madam.*

4 Think about register

Tick (✓) the option in the pairs of phrases or sentences below which is more appropriate to use in a formal letter expressing an opinion.

1 **a** What I think is …
b It seems to me that …

2 **a** It is nonsense to say …
b I am not convinced when people say …

3 **a** Being able to access information instantly is invaluable.
b It is great to know we can get information on the spot.

4 **a** Something else you have got to remember is that …
b A second point to bear in mind is that …

5 **a** It is now widely accepted that …
b Most of us know that …

Factfile

The Internet, also known as cyberspace, is a network of people and information linked together by telephone lines. It allows people using computers around the world to exchange information more easily and in greater quantities than ever before. Computer users who have an e-mail address can exchange e-mails (electronic messages). E-mail has become a very popular form of communication between friends, family, and especially businesses; it is fast, cost-effective and reliable.

The Internet also allows users to go onto the World Wide Web. This is a multimedia resource and communications tool, and allows people to access and exchange text, images, video and audio files by downloading them onto their computer. Internet users can also access chat rooms, forums or newsrooms, where they can exchange ideas and information with people they have never met, anywhere in the world.

5 Brainstorm the topic

Work with a partner and answer the questions. Note down the best ideas.

1 Look at the exam question. Are you surprised at the results of the survey? Why/Why not?

2 In your opinion, why are young people spending more and more time in front of a computer screen? To access information for their studies? For some other reason? Is this a good thing?

3 If you were cautioning young people about the amount of time they spend using computers, what would you warn about? Health risks? The risk of becoming addicted to computer games or the Internet? Other problems?

4 Do you think it is important for young people to read books? Why/Why not?

5 Would it be a good idea to attempt to read a whole book off a computer screen? Why/Why not?

6 Under what circumstances might it be better to read a book rather than use a computer?

7 Under what circumstances might it be better to use a computer rather than read a book?

8 Do you think computers could ever replace books? Why/Why not?

6 Organise your notes

a Look at the way one student organised his notes after a brainstorming session. Organise the ideas *you* brainstormed above into similar topic areas.

Why are young people using computers more?
- to access information for studies (World Wide Web/Internet etc.)
- to e-mail/communicate across the world
- to play games
- computers are becoming cheaper to buy
- access to a computer is easy

Problems
- overuse of computers can be anti-social
- children don't go out with friends any more
- children can access unsuitable material over the Internet
- computer games and the Internet can be addictive
- neck/back/eye problems if computer used over long periods
- not everyone can afford a computer

Why are people not reading books so much?
- can get information from Internet rather than libraries
- multimedia have greater appeal than books
- less time available

How important are books?
- books are cheaper and more accessible
- reading books is better over long periods, doesn't involve staring at screen
- important to keep habit of sustained reading to avoid falling standards of literacy
- it's easier to relax with a book

Which is preferable?
- both are important and necessary

tip

Organising your ideas and notes into topic areas will help you to paragraph a text correctly.

exam tip

In the exam, your letter must be between 300 and 350 words, so you may not be able to include all the ideas you have brainstormed. If you think you have too many ideas, go through them and cross out those that are less important or relevant.

b Look again at the writer's notes above. Put a cross (**✗**) against any that you think could or should be omitted.

7 Read a model letter

a Read the model letter below and compare it with the notes the writer made in **6a** above. Which notes did the writer *not* use in his letter?

Dear Sir or Madam,

I watched your recent programme and was interested to learn the results of the survey you carried out. I was particularly interested in your findings regarding the increased use of computers and the decline in book reading.

The fact that more young people are using computers is hardly surprising. The development of the World Wide Web has meant that we can now access a wealth of information quickly and easily without leaving our homes. This facility is invaluable to students and should, of course, be welcomed. Computers can also be used for easy, cheap communication across the world, which has benefited millions and brought people closer together.

However, there are reasons why computers can never replace books. First of all, while computers are clearly indispensable when it comes to finding facts, they are not suitable for prolonged periods of reading. When you settle down to a book, you need to spend time reflecting on what the writer is saying. You cannot do this easily when you read text off a screen. A second point to remember is that there are many situations where we can read books but we cannot access a computer. If we lose the habit of reading books, we will not be able to take advantage of this opportunity.

Another reason for not using computers for sustained periods of reading is for health reasons. Doctors warn that staring at a screen for hours is harmful – it affects the eyesight, and can cause back and neck problems. It cannot be good for young people to risk their health in this way.

A final consideration is the amount of time some people spend playing computer games. For some young people, it can become an addiction. Addicts waste time and money and become increasingly cut off from friends. By forgoing exercise, they also damage their health.

I do not for a moment dispute the necessity for young people to use computers but neither must they lose touch with the printed book. If young people lose the habit of reading in this way, I believe it will be a negative and worrying development for our society.

b Has the writer covered all the points asked for in the exam question? Has he used the correct format, style and tone?

c Has the writer paragraphed his letter appropriately? Write a brief summary of each paragraph in the spaces below.

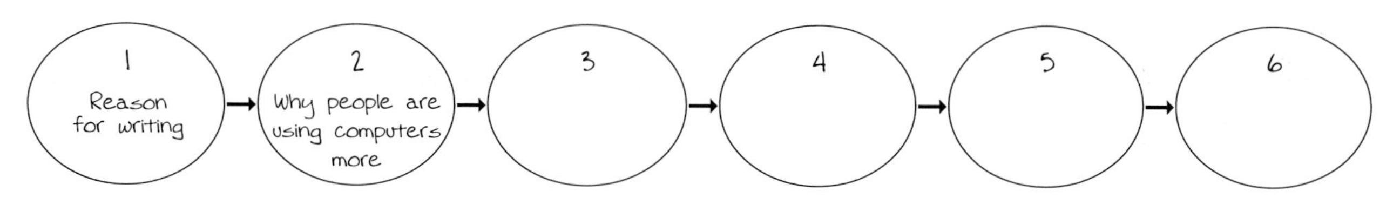

d Underline the topic sentences in each paragraph of the model letter.

8 Think about language

Collocations

a Match the verbs (1–6) that collocate with the nouns (a–f).

1 carry out	**a** games
2 access	**b** your health
3 spend	**c** a finding
4 damage/risk	**d** a habit
5 play	**e** a survey
6 form	**f** information
7 dispute	**g** time

b Find words or phrases in the model text that mean the same as the words in italics.

1 I was interested in *the things that you found out.*
2 The survey showed a *decrease* in book reading.
3 With a computer, you can obtain *a huge amount of* information.
4 Computers and the World Wide Web are *extremely useful.*
5 Computers are *impossible to manage without.*
6 Computers are not suitable for *long, continuous* periods of reading.
7 When you read a book, you need to spend time *thinking* about what the writer is saying.
8 By *going without* exercise, you can damage your health.

9 Think about linking words

a Look at the model letter in **7** above. Underline the phrases the writer uses to list points in his argument. Can you suggest an alternative for each phrase?

b Join the following sentences in as many ways as possible, using the words in the box.

while/although **however/nevertheless** **despite the fact that** **in spite of the fact that**

1 Computers are now essential to our lives. They will never replace books.
2 You can look up facts in a book. The process is much quicker on the Internet.
3 It is true that computers make information easily accessible. Readers can't relax with a computer in the same way as with a book.

10 Exam practice: Write a letter giving an opinion

You are going to write a letter giving an opinion. Read the exam question and follow the instructions below.

Part 2

Write your answer in **300–350 words** in an appropriate style.

A radio programme has conducted a survey of young people's television viewing habits. As a result, they have established that young people are spending more time in front of a screen, either watching TV or playing computer games, than doing sport or socialising with friends. Readers have been asked to write in to the programme suggesting why this is happening, saying how serious they think the problem is, and what they think should be done about it.

Write your **letter**. Do not write any postal addresses.

- **Identify the key points in the question**
  Underline the points you have to cover in the exam question.
- **Brainstorm the topic**
  Note down ideas and make a plan before you begin to write.
- **Organise your notes**
  Group your ideas/notes into topic areas.
- **Think about paragraphing**
  Start a new paragraph for each new topic area. Write a topic sentence for each paragraph.
- **Think about linking words**
  Use linking words and phrases like 'Firstly', 'Another point to consider is …' to list points in your argument.

6 Describing an experience

1 Read the question

Read the exam question below carefully.

Part 2

Write your answer in **300–350 words** in an appropriate style.

A travel magazine has asked readers for contributions for a special holiday edition entitled 'A Great Way to Travel!' Write an article describing a trip you have made that was both pleasurable and eventful, giving reasons for your chosen means of transport.

Write your **article**.

exam information

Articles may occur in both parts of the Writing Paper. In the exam, you may be asked to write an article describing an experience you have had, such as a holiday or a journey.

2 Think about your reader

Look at the exam question again and answer the following questions.

1 What kind of publication will your article appear in?

2 What is the title of the special edition you are writing for? Underline it.

3 For what purpose are you writing the article? (More than one answer is possible.)
- **a** to describe a trip on which a lot of different things happened
- **b** to compare different forms of transport
- **c** to explain why you chose to travel in a certain way
- **d** for some other reason

4 What do you know about the readers of the publication you are writing for?
- **a** nothing at all
- **b** they are all young people
- **c** nothing, except that they are interested in travel
- **d** they are fellow students

3 Identify the key points in the question

Look at the exam question again and answer the following questions.

1 Could the trip you describe have been boring? Could it have been disastrous? Underline the two adjectives in the exam question which tell you what kind of trip you must describe.

2 What must you do in your article in addition to describing your trip?

4 Brainstorm the topic

Work with a partner and answer the questions. Note down the best ideas.

1 If you were making the trip of a lifetime, where would you go? Why?

2 What form of transport would you take? Why?

3 What's the most pleasurable/eventful trip you have ever made? How did you travel? Where did you go? What did you see? What happened on the way – something exciting or unexpected? What made it so pleasurable?

5 Think about a title

a Match the titles (1–5) with sentences from the opening paragraphs (a–e) of various articles.

1 Desert Adventure
2 Danger in the Skies
3 Alone in a White Wilderness
4 Stranded!
5 Money to Burn

tip

Titles for newspaper and magazine articles are short and pithy. They should capture the central theme of the article in a few, well-chosen words. Notice that adjectives, nouns and past participles are commonly used.

a Just imagine you are travelling through some remote corner of the world. You hop off the train at a small station to buy something to eat, only to find on your return that the train has departed. There is no sign of habitation for miles. This, of course, is exactly what happened to me.

b Who in their right mind would choose to cross the snowy wastes of Alaska on foot and with only a pack of Huskies for company?

c Supposing you had won the lottery and had one million dollars at your disposal. What would you do first?

d Have you ever asked yourself what you would do if the plane you were travelling on was hijacked?

e When a friend invited me to join him on a trek across the Sahara, I presumed he had gone insane.

b Now look at the exam question again and write down two possible titles for *your* article.

6 Think about your introduction

Look at the exam question again, then read the three introductory paragraphs (a–c) below. Which paragraph would make a good introduction? Why? What is wrong with the others? Use this guide to help you.

A good introductory paragraph to an article should:

- be relevant and to the point.
- grab the reader's interest.
- be longer than one sentence in length but should not be 'waffle' (a long stream of words that do not say anything important).

a

One of the biggest problems about planning a trip, whether it be for pleasure or for work, is to decide how to travel. You have to decide whether a plane is too expensive compared to a train and whether a coach will take too long. I had just this problem when I decided to travel across Europe last summer and it took me a very long time to make up my mind how to travel because there were advantages and disadvantages to a lot of different forms of transport, so it was hard to decide.

b

If you were planning a trip to some far-flung corner of the globe, what means of travel would you choose? Would you be one of those intrepid types who set off with nothing but a backpack, a map, and a prayer? Would you whiz across the globe on a supersonic jet? Or would you opt for a long, languorous sea crossing on a luxury cruise liner?

c

Last year I went on a trip that was both pleasurable and memorable and I would recommend it to all the readers of this magazine.

7 Think about your conclusion

Look at the exam question again, then read the three concluding paragraphs (a–c) below. Which paragraph would make a good conclusion? Why? What is wrong with the others?
Use this guide to help you.

A good concluding paragraph to an article should:

- give the reader a sense of closure.
- carry a punch, instead of ending in a boring and totally predictable way.
- be longer than one sentence in length.

a

So take a tip from me when you come to plan your grand tour. If you want to savour the experience to the full, while having the time of your life, take the train. You don't believe me? Just try it for yourself. I guarantee you won't be disappointed.

b

To sum up, my trip was pleasurable and eventful and I think I chose the best way to travel. I think any reader who wants to travel should do what I did.

c

We spent the last part of our trip on a beach in Thailand. We arrived home from our trip after midnight and we had to start work the next day, so we were very tired.

8 Read a model article

a Read the model article below. Then use these questions to help you to decide if the writer has produced a good text.

Has the writer:

1 covered all aspects of the exam question?
2 written too few words? (Don't count them, just estimate.)
3 written anything that could be considered irrelevant?
4 forgotten to start a new paragraph for each change of topic?
5 written topic sentences for each paragraph?
6 written any one-sentence paragraphs?
7 developed each of her paragraphs?
8 used mainly vocabulary that is very basic in level?
9 made a lot of simple grammar or spelling mistakes?
10 punctuated the article correctly?

The Journey of a Lifetime

If you were planning a trip to some far-flung corner of the globe, what means of travel would you choose? Would you be one of those intrepid types who set off with nothing but a backpack, a map, and a prayer? Would you whiz across the globe on a supersonic jet? Or would you opt for a long, languorous sea crossing on a luxury cruise liner?

Before setting off for India, we agonised long and hard over the best way to travel. Chris, my travelling companion, suggested we fly direct (at bucket shop prices of course!) and then backpack across the country. Backpacking appealed to me, but not flying. I was dying to travel overland across Europe and Asia and experience the sights, smells and sounds of each different country. Hitch-hiking was a seductive idea but it was also potentially risky. So what form of transport would offer us flexibility and adventure without risk? Coach travel was unappealing. In the end, there was only one option. We took the train.

Did the trip measure up to our expectations? You bet it did! There is something incredibly exciting about boarding a night train and waking up in a different country. We rattled through valleys and over mountains, peering through grimy windows at the stunning scenery. We visited ruins steeped in history and bustling, modern cities. And we had adventures galore. In Italy, we fell in with some locals who were celebrating a village festival. We partied for hours and, when everyone had gone home, we camped out under the stars. In Russia we got lost while we were visiting the Kremlin and were nearly arrested for vagrancy!

We became impervious to the vicissitudes of train travel. Roasting in sweltering compartments by day and shivering in unheated carriages by night all seemed part of the adventure. We learnt to cope with the vagaries of foreign timetables and became adept at communicating by means of hand signals. By the time we reached India, we were already seasoned travellers.

So take a tip from me when you come to plan your grand tour. If you want to savour the experience to the full, while having the time of your life, take the train. You don't believe me? Just try it for yourself. I guarantee you won't be disappointed.

b Now study the list below. It includes some of the features of a well-written article. Find examples of these in the model article in **a**.

A well-written article:

- usually has an appropriate title.
- often addresses the reader directly.
- has a lively tone.
- is vivid and descriptive.
- appeals to the reader's imagination.
- draws on the writer's personal experience.
- may include narrative tenses.
- often contains rhetorical questions.
- is often semi-formal.

c Write a brief summary of each paragraph of the model article in the spaces below.

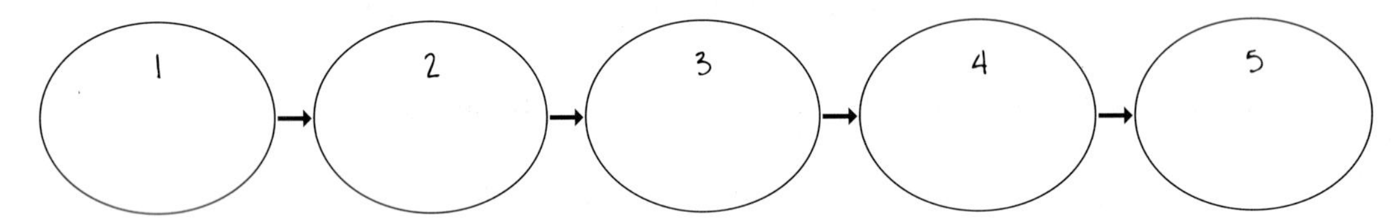

9 Think about vocabulary

Find words or phrases in the model article which mean the same as the words in italics.

1 Could you be described as *willing to go to dangerous or unknown places?*
2 Many travellers simply *move very fast* through the countries they are visiting.
3 She doesn't like trains, so I think she will *choose* another means of transport.
4 The explorer *deliberated for a long time* on the best way to travel.
5 Have you ever bought tickets from a *business that sells cheap tickets for air travel.*
6 The traveller found one of his companion's suggestions very *attractive and tempting.*
7 I will be very disappointed if the voyage does not *match* my expectations.
8 The Mediterranean is a part of the world that is *full of historical interest.*
9 I really suffer in the heat, but my travelling companion is *not affected by* any form of physical discomfort.
10 The *unexpected changes* of the weather meant that they travelled slowly.

10 Think about grammar

Gerund or infinitive

Complete the following sentences with the correct form of the verb in brackets.

1 I'm dying .... (go) on a cruise round the Arctic to see the wildlife there.
2 Shall we get the train or would you prefer .... (hop on) this coach?
3 Before .... (set off), we planned our itinerary meticulously.
4 Chris suggested .... (fly) to India and then backpacking across the country.
5 If you could tour the world, how would you opt .... (travel)?
6 .... (backpack) doesn't really appeal to me.
7 I don't think I'd choose .... (settle) in a really cold country.
8 Try .... (travel) by train and you'll soon realise why it's better than flying.

11 Think about tenses

a Tick (✓) the tenses and structures that you would probably use in describing aspects of a past experience. How many of the ones you have ticked are used in the model article?

1 Past Simple
2 Past Continuous
3 Present Perfect Simple
4 Present Perfect Continuous
5 Present Simple
6 Past Perfect Simple
7 Past Perfect Continuous
8 Third Conditional

b Complete the following sentences with the correct form of the verb in brackets.

1 By the time we .... (arrive) at our destination, we .... (spend) all our money.
2 The train .... (stop) suddenly while we .... (go) through the tunnel.
3 The train .... (halt) at the border town and a customs official .... (check) our passports.
4 We .... (wait) for a full three hours by the time the train .... (pull) into the station.
5 Someone .... (stole) money out of my rucksack while I .... (sleep).
6 By the end of the first day, we .... (eat) all the food we .... (take) with us.

12 Exam practice: Write an article describing an experience

You are going to write an article describing an experience. Read the exam question and follow the instructions below.

Part 2

Write your answer in **300–350 words** in an appropriate style.

A weekly newspaper is running a 'Foreign Travel' page and has invited contributions from readers. Write an article describing a trip you have made abroad that was enjoyable and eventful, explaining why you chose your particular destination.

Write your **article**.

- **Think about a title**
  Give your article an interesting title.
- **Think about your introduction**
  Get your readers' attention by making your introduction as vivid and interesting as possible.
- **Think about your conclusion**
  Your conclusion should round off your article well. Allow yourself time to write a good concluding paragraph.
- **Think about style**
  Make your article vivid by addressing your reader directly. Asking rhetorical questions may help you to do this.
- **Edit your text**
  When you finish your article, remember to check your grammar, spelling and punctuation. Then try exchanging your work with someone else in your class. Comment on each other's work, using the guides on p.40 and p.42 to help you.

7 Describing an event

1 Read the question

Read the exam question below carefully.

Part 2

Write your answer in **300–350 words** in an appropriate style.

A quality monthly magazine is looking for articles to publish on its 'Marriage – Past and Present' page. Write an article describing a memorable wedding you have attended and compare it with the sort of wedding your great-grandparents might have had. Say whether you think the weddings of today reflect changes that have taken place in the institution of marriage in recent years.

Write your **article**.

exam information

In the exam, you may be asked to write an article describing an event, such as a festival or a wedding.

2 Think about your reader

Look at the exam question again and answer the following questions.

1 What sort of publication are you writing for?

2 What do you know about the people who are going to read your article?
- **a** they are fellow students
- **b** they are academics
- **c** nothing at all

3 For what purpose are you writing the article? To criticise something? To describe something? For some other reason?

3 Identify the key points in the question

Look at the exam question again and answer the following questions.

1 What is the title of the page you are writing for? Underline it.

2 What kind of ceremony are you asked to describe? Could the ceremony you describe have been boring? Underline the adjective in the exam question which tells you this.

3 You are asked to do *three* things in your article. What are they?

Factfile

The institution of marriage has undergone a number of changes over the past century. Our great-grandparents would have expected a wedding to begin with a religious service, which may have taken place in a temple, mosque, synagogue or church. When the groom vowed to take the bride as his 'lawfully wedded wife', he was making a very firm commitment. His bride took the same vow in her turn. The bonds of matrimony were considered sacred and it was rare for a couple to seek divorce, which carried a stigma in the close-knit communities most people lived in.

In some countries, dynastic marriages were arranged to forge bonds between leading families. It was expected that a wife would bring a dowry (property and/or money) to her spouse on marriage.

Today, many young couples marry in a registry office, having opted for a civil service rather than a religious one. People live in nuclear families nowadays rather than the extended families of old, so families have less say in who their children marry. Divorce is far more common than in the past. Some young people have turned their backs on the institution of marriage and live together as common-law partners. There is also an increasing number of single parents, who have no partner and bring up their children alone.

4 Think about vocabulary

a Complete the following sentences with a suitable word or phrase from the box.

best man bride bridesmaids groom hen
honeymoon reception registry office stag

1. At a wedding, the woman who is to be married is called the ....bride................ and the man is called the ......groom............ .
2. The ....best.....man...... acts as chief supporter to the man who is about to be married.
3. The woman's attendants are called ...bridesmaids... . They are often quite young and usually wear special dresses.
4. Some days before the wedding, a man may have a ....hen.......... party to mark the end of his life as a bachelor; a woman may have a ......stag............... party.
5. People usually get married in a place of worship or at a ...registry....office... .
6. The party after the wedding is called the ...reception........... .
7. After the wedding, the newly-weds usually go on a .....honeymoon..... .

b Complete the following sentences with the correct form of a suitable verb from the box.

conduct exchange get hold make propose

1 My cousin .... married a few weeks ago.
2 The local vicar .... the wedding service.
3 In the church, the bride and bridegroom .... vows.
4 The reception .... in a large hotel.
5 The bridegroom .... a speech in which he praised his new bride.
6 Then the best man .... a toast to the newly married couple.

c Complete the following sentences with a suitable word from the box.

close-knit commitment extended forge sacred single spouse stigma vows

1 The couple came from a(n) .... community, where everyone knew each other well.
2 Long ago, marriage often helped to .... bonds between two dynasties.
3 In former times, parents, grandparents and children lived together in .... families.
4 Barbara isn't married; she's a(n) .... parent.
5 These days, people often break the .... they made when they got married.
6 Some young people see marriage as a huge .... which they would prefer to avoid.
7 Many people believe marriage is a(n) .... institution.
8 In the past, women often stayed with their .... because they wished to avoid the .... of divorce.

tip

When you describe a scene, imagine you are a film cameraman. You don't want to film all the unimportant details. Zoom in on the most interesting features and events and capture them vividly for your reader.

5 Brainstorm the topic

Work with a partner. Discuss these questions and note down the best ideas.

1 In what ways has the institution of marriage changed in the past hundred years?
2 Is your attitude to marriage similar to or different from that of your parents or your grandparents?
3 Have you ever been to a wedding? Where was the wedding held? Was the ceremony traditional or modern? Describe the wedding and the main participants.
4 Did you enjoy the wedding? What did you like/not like about it?
5 Would you like the same sort of ceremony yourself (assuming you are not already married)?
6 How do you think the wedding compared with the sort of wedding your great-grandparents might have had?
7 In your article, you have to describe a memorable wedding. Was the wedding you attended memorable? If not, what kind of wedding you think would be more memorable?

6 Make a plan

a Select ideas that you want to include in your article, and make notes, grouping related ideas into topic areas.

b Look at the plan below and decide if it would be suitable for *your* article.

Paragraph 1 (Introduction): Are weddings different from how they used to be?

Paragraph 2: The wedding I attended - who? where? when? The ceremony.

Paragraph 3: What happened after the ceremony? Why was the day enjoyable/memorable?

Paragraph 4 (Conclusion): Compare weddings today with weddings in the past. Do changes reflect modern attitudes to institution of marriage?

7 Think about your introduction

Look at the exam question again, then read the three introductory paragraphs (a–c) below. Which paragraph would make a good introduction? Why? What is wrong with the others? Use this guide to help you:

A good introduction to an article:

- awakens your interest and makes you want to read the rest of the article.
- focuses on the theme of the article.
- contains a number of sentences that are well linked.
- contains sentences that develop one central idea.
- may pose a question or appeal to the reader's imagination.
- leads easily into the next paragraph/the rest of the article.

a Marriage has changed a great deal and this has had an effect on the sort of weddings people have.

b These days many people don't see marriage as a sacred institution, so they don't bother getting married in church and in fact some people don't want to get married at all because they think it's just a piece of paper and they don't want all that commitment so they just live together without getting married. It was all very different in the past.

c Where do you fancy getting married? Maybe you favour a traditional ceremony in a church or mosque, or a secular, registry office wedding. Or are you one of those unconventional types who would prefer to exchange vows underwater or hanging from a parachute? In former times, marriage was a highly respected institution and as a result, weddings were performed with some solemnity. And now? Well, these days many people take a more relaxed view of marriage and this is reflected in the sort of weddings they have.

8 Read a model article

a One of the paragraphs in **7** forms the introduction of the article below. Read that paragraph again. Then read the rest of the article and suggest a suitable title.

Take my cousin's wedding for example. *It* took place on the lawns of a luxury hotel. The guests, numbering about fifty in all, sat in rows in front of an altar, the sides of *which* were elaborately decked with ribbons and garlands. After a suitable delay, the wedding march struck up and the bride glided towards us through a flowered arch, smiling shyly at the assembled company. The bridegroom, who was waiting at the altar, turned and beamed at her. Soon, the wedding ceremony was under way.

So much for innovation, you may think. But wait! No sooner had the couple taken their vows than the ribbons and garlands were whisked from the altar – to reveal the basket of a hot air balloon. Just imagine our surprise when the newly-weds stepped into *it* and were borne away into the sunset, the picture of romantic bliss! Later, when *they* had regained terra firma and the reception was in full swing, I got the chance to ride in the hot air balloon. *It* was exciting, invigorating – and extremely romantic! As weddings go, *this one* was definitely memorable!

So how does all *this* compare with the sort of wedding our great-grandparents might have celebrated? *It* was definitely less conventional but when it comes down to it, the ceremony was, in essence, much the same as *it* has always been: a man and a woman exchanging vows in front of friends and family. To that extent at least, nothing much has changed.

b Look at the model article again and answer the following questions.

1 In an article, the writer often addresses the reader directly. Find examples in the model text.
2 An article may have (rhetorical) questions. Find examples in the model text.
3 A well-written article is lively in tone. Is this true of the model, in your opinion?
4 An article is often semi-formal in tone, rather than very formal. In what tone is this article written? Pick out phrases which illustrate this.
5 A good article often draws on the writer's personal experience. Does the model text do this?
6 An article often requires a range of narrative tenses. Find examples in the model text?
7 A good article will contain a good range of appropriate vocabulary. Does the model article contain a good range? Find examples in the model text.

9 Think about language

Find words and phrases in the model article (including the introduction) which mean the same as the following.

1 seriousness ....
2 decorated ....
3 started playing ....
4 smiled broadly ....
5 new idea(s) ....
6 joy and happiness ....
7 landed on the ground ....
8 at its highest level of activity ....

10 Think about reference words

Look back at the model article on p.47. The words in italics all refer back to words or ideas used earlier in the text. Which words or ideas do they refer back to?

11 Think about sentence structure

Join the following sentences using participle clauses.

e.g. The guests numbered about fifty in all. They sat in rows.
The guests, numbering about fifty in all, sat in rows.

I looked round. I noticed that some of the guests were wearing hats.
Looking round, I noticed that some of the guests were wearing hats.

1 The bride arrived. She was smiling shyly.
....
2 The bridegroom was standing near the altar. He was waiting for her.
....
3 I felt hot. I went to sit in the shade.
....
4 After the vicar had finished the service, he left the church.
....
5 The newly-weds waved to the guests. They sailed away in their balloon.
....
6 I hoped to get something to eat. I went towards the refreshment tent.
....

exam tip

Examiners award marks for the correct and appropriate use of complex sentence structures, so don't just use simple sentences in your article.

12 Make your article vivid

You can make your article more vivid by asking rhetorical questions and appealing to the reader's imagination. Rewrite the following sentences, beginning with the words given.

e.g It must feel fantastic to go up in a hot air balloon.
Imagine *how fantastic it must feel to go up in a hot air balloon.*
Can you imagine *how fantastic it must feel to go up in a hot air balloon?*

1 We were amazed when we realised what was happening.
Can you imagine ....

2 The newly-weds were delighted when they heard the news.
Imagine ....

3 The guests were astonished.
Picture to yourself ....

4 Have you ever been to a really unconventional wedding?
I wonder if ....

5 I wonder what our grandparents would have made of modern weddings.
So what ...., I wonder?

13 Exam practice: Write an article describing an event

You are going to write an article describing an event. Read the exam question and follow the instructions below.

Part 2

Write your answer in **300–350 words** in an appropriate style.

A weekly magazine is asking readers to contribute articles for a special feature entitled 'Festivals Round the World'. Write an article describing a festival you have taken part in that was both memorable and enjoyable and say whether you think the celebration of such festivals has any relevance for people today.

Write your **article**.

- **Think about a title**
  Remember to give your article an original title.
- **Think about style and tone**
  Do not use too formal a style. You need to engage with your readers and address them directly.
- **Think about paragraphing**
  Remember to paragraph your article appropriately.
- **Think about your introduction**
  Make your first paragraph vivid. Appeal to the reader's imagination.
- **Think about tenses**
  Use a good range of narrative tenses.
- **Think about sentence structure**
  Use a good range of different structures to make your article more interesting.

8 Discussing benefits and drawbacks

exam information

In Part 1 of the Writing Paper, articles will have a discursive function, e.g. you may be asked consider the advantages (the pros/benefits) and disadvantages (the cons/drawbacks) of a situation.

1 Read the question

Read the exam question below carefully.

Part 1

You **must** answer this question. Write your answer in **300–350** words in an appropriate style.

Recently, a leading politician was asked to give her views on the development of tourism. She was quoted in a national newspaper as saying:

> 'Over recent decades, tourism has undoubtedly benefited both the holiday maker and the host country. The economic benefits are obvious. But it is now time to take stock. Tourism affects local communities and also wildlife in ways that are unpredictable and not always positive. We must ask ourselves whether tourism on the scale we have it now is a blessing or a curse.'

As a follow up, a tourist magazine plans to publish a series of articles exploring the benefits and drawbacks of tourism. Write an article for the magazine, giving your opinion and commenting on the politician's statement above.

Write your **article**.

2 Think about your reader

Work with a partner. Look at the instructions (rubric) in the exam question again and answer the following questions.

1 Whose opinion is expressed in the quotation? Where did you come across the quotation?

2 Who is going to publish articles about the pros and cons of tourism?

3 Who is going to read your article?

4 Why are you writing the article? To argue against tourism? To comment on what the speaker said? To consider the advantages and disadvantages of tourism?

3 Identify the key points in the question

Work with a partner. Look at the quotation in the exam question again and answer the following questions.

1 Does the speaker think that tourism has been a good thing over the last few decades?
2 What does she mean when she says 'it is now time to take stock'?
   a It is time to stop tourism.
   b It is time to consider the situation and what to do next.
3 Who has benefited from tourism, according to the speaker?
4 Who has probably benefited economically?
5 Who or what else is affected by tourism? How? Underline one adjective and one phrase which the speaker uses to describe these effects.
6 What question does the speaker say we must ask ourselves? What does she mean by 'on the scale we have it now'?
7 Is a 'blessing' a good thing or a bad thing? What about a 'curse'?

4 Think about register

Now study the list below. Which of the features would be inappropriate in the article you are going to write? Put a cross (✗) next to them.

- a formal, scientific style
- clear paragraphs
- topic sentences
- a lot of very basic sentence structures
- slang
- rhetorical questions
- a wide range of appropriate vocabulary
- an original title
- an opening such as 'To Whom it May Concern'

Factfile

In recent years, more and more people have become aware of the negative effects of tourism and the ecological and social damage it may cause. There has been a call for a new orientation in tourist policies. Those who have espoused the idea of eco-tourism believe that policies for tourism should not be based on economic and technological considerations alone but should also take into account environmental conservation and the needs of local host populations.

8 Discussing benefits and drawbacks

5 Brainstorm the topic

Work with a partner and answer the questions. Note down the best ideas.

1. How do you think tourism benefits holiday makers? Make a list. e.g. *It offers the chance of rest and relaxation.*
2. What benefits does tourism bring to host countries? Make a list. e.g. *It brings in money.*
3. In what ways can tourism benefit wildlife?
4. What negative effects can it have on wildlife?
5. In what ways can tourism benefit local communities?
6. What negative effects can it have on local communities? (Think of local people living in or near a big, new resort.)
7. In what way can the effects of tourism be 'unpredictable'? Can you think of some concrete examples?
8. Do you think that tourism on its present scale is a blessing or a curse?

6 Make a plan

a Look at the following notes which one student has made for the exam question. Put a cross (✗) against any points that are irrelevant or unimportant.

- a history of tourism
- how to attract more tourists to our region
- how money from tourism can be used to preserve animal habitats
- description of my last holiday
- how tourism helps the local economy
- types of pollution caused by tourism
- eco-tourism
- what happens when resorts impinge on wildlife e.g. turtle beaches threatened
- the unforeseen consequences of tourism e.g. new roads/airports and their effect on environment

b Look at each of these possible outlines for your article and put the items in a suitable order.

A

- a section (of one paragraph or more) which deals with the negative or unpredictable aspects of tourism ☐
- one paragraph that leads into the topic [1]
- a section (of one paragraph or more) which deals with the positive aspects of tourism ☐
- one paragraph that sums up what has been said ☐

B

- one paragraph that sums up what has been said ☐
- a section (of one paragraph or more) which deals with the first set of positive and related negative/unpredictable effects of tourism ☐
- one paragraph that leads into the topic ☐
- a section (of one paragraph or more) which deals with the next set of positive and related negative/unpredictable effects of tourism ☐

c Look at the notes you made when you brainstormed the question. Make a plan for your article based on one of the outlines in **b**.

Plan

Paragraph 1: Inroduction: The fact that tourism can be both beneficial and harmful.

Paragraph 2: ....

Paragraph 3: ....

Paragraph 4: ....

exam tip

Organise your ideas *before* you start writing. If you don't, your article will be confusing and difficult to follow. The examiner will award points for good organisation. Do not include irrelevant points. You will be penalised if you do so.

7 Think about style

When you make statements, be careful not to over-generalise. The statements below are over-generalisations. Rewrite the sentences in a more tentative way.

e.g. Everybody takes foreign holidays these days.
Many people take foreign holidays these days.

1 Tourists have no respect for the environment.

2 Holiday makers are rowdy and unpleasant.

3 Developers always build hotels in environmentally sensitive places.

4 Tourism brings wealth to a poor area.

5 People don't care about the environment nowadays.

8 Read a model article

a Read the model article below and say which outline, A or B in **6a** above, the writer used.

Tourism: a Blessing or a Curse?

Where did you spend your last holidays? Did you sunbathe on a foreign beach or go sightseeing in some historic city? It seems we have all become tourists, rushing off on weekend excursions and package holidays. The tourist industry is booming, but should we be pleased or worried about its effects?

Let's begin with the positive side. First of all, surely nobody would disagree with the statement that tourism benefits both the holiday maker and the host country. Travel broadens the mind, encouraging tolerance and understanding between peoples. Second, tourism provides employment and can contribute significantly to the economy of a country. This is of particular importance in poor developing countries. The income generated by tourism helps to pay for education, hospitals, roads and airports. Finally, tourism can benefit wildlife. When local people realise that tourists will pay to see animals in their natural habitats, they are more inclined to protect these creatures rather than hunt and kill them.

If there are so many benefits to tourism, what's the problem? Well, it is certainly true that the effects of tourism can be unpredictable. To begin with, tourism can ruin an area of beauty, especially when over-development is allowed. We have all heard of resorts that are overrun with rowdy, unpleasant holiday makers. In some cases, the yearly invasion can be so bad that local people have had to move away. Another concern is the effect of tourism on wildlife. We are disrupting the lives of animals in many ways, whether by noise, disturbance or pollution. Think, for example, of the beaches used by turtles over thousands of years that have now been ruined by developers.

So is tourism a blessing or a curse? The answer must be that it is both. Part of the problem is that the results of tourist activity are sometimes unpredictable. The fact that developers do not mean to wipe out an endangered species from the face of the earth does not make the event any less tragic. Perhaps we need to become more responsible as tourists and subscribe to the spread of eco-tourism. If we give more consideration to the impact of our activities on the places we visit, we can go some way to lessening the worst effects of tourism.

b Look back at the model article in **a**. Then go through this list and tick the appropriate column. Has the writer succeeded in writing a good article?

1	Is the text set out as an article?	Yes ☐	No ☐
2	Is it written in an appropriate style and tone?	Yes ☐	No ☐
3	Has the writer forgotten to give the article a title?	Yes ☐	No ☐
4	Does the article appeal directly to the reader?	Yes ☐	No ☐
5	Is it difficult to follow?	Yes ☐	No ☐
6	Is it organised into clear paragraphs?	Yes ☐	No ☐
7	Has the writer used one of the outlines in 6b?	Yes ☐	No ☐
8	Does each paragraph introduce and develop a fresh topic?	Yes ☐	No ☐
9	Has the writer forgotten to include a topic sentence in each paragraph? (Underline the topic sentences you can find.)	Yes ☐	No ☐
10	Does the writer expand on, explain or illustrate the topic sentence in each paragraph?	Yes ☐	No ☐
11	Does the writer discuss the benefits *and* the drawbacks of tourism?	Yes ☐	No ☐
12	Does the writer give sufficient weight to both sides of the question?	Yes ☐	No ☐

9 Think about vocabulary

a Find words and phrases in the model letter which mean the same as the words in italics.

1 The tourist industry *is flourishing.*

2 It's a thrill to see animals in *the places where they live naturally.*

3 Some tourists are unwelcome because they are *very badly-behaved and noisy.*

4 Tourism is *disturbing* the lives of people in many small communities.

5 Developers may *cause* an endangered species *to become extinct.*

6 People are becoming aware of the need to *support* eco-tourism.

7 Large-scale tourism can have an unpredictable *effect* on a small community.

8 We can go some way to *decreasing* the worst effects of tourism.

Collocations

b Match the words (1–6) that collocate with the words (a–f). (Sometimes there is more than one answer.)

1 weekend	a excursion
2 endangered	b habitat
3 holiday	c holiday
4 natural	d industry
5 package	e resort
6 tourist	f species

c Complete the following sentences with a suitable preposition.

1 Next year, we are planning to go .... a package holiday to Bali.

2 Tourism brings .... a lot of money.

3 Tourism helps to pay .... basic services in many poor countries.

4 A number of factors have contributed .... the increase in tourism in recent years.

5 Sometimes tourism depends .... the animals in that area.

6 The effect of tourism .... wildlife must be considered.

7 The island is overrun .... tourists, especially in the months of July and August.

8 The new airport has had a huge impact .... the bird life in the area.

10 Think about language

a The phrases below are often found in 'for and against' texts. Underline the phrases the writer uses in the model article.

Let's begin with the positive side. One of the benefits/advantages of ... is ... This means that ... This is of particular importance to/in ... It seems that ... One problem is that ...	Another concern is that ... This is due to ... Think, for example, of ... The answer must be that it is ... Part of the problem is that ... Perhaps we all need to ...

b How many of the linking words and phrases below occurred in the model article? Underline them. Can you add any more items to each list?

Sequencing ideas

Introductory phrases

To begin with, …

First and foremost, …

In the second place, …

Next, …

Another point to consider is …

Finally, …

Last but not least, …

Concluding phrases

To sum up, it seems that …

In conclusion, it appears that …

Overall, I would say that …

Adding information

besides, …

furthermore, …

moreover, …

tip

Use linking words and phrases in your writing where appropriate but don't overuse them or your text will sound strange.

11 Edit a text

The following article contains some basic errors, which a teacher has marked. Rewrite the article correctly using her code to help you.

G - grammar	P - punctuation	PARA - new paragraph
T - tense	PREP - preposition	WF - wrong form
WW - wrong word	SP - spelling	

Have you ever been on holiday, or on a brief excursion to a place of interest? If so, you are one of the millions of tourists that this article is aimed [PREP] on. Between us, we tourists [T] created a growing industry that has changed the lives of many, many people. But are these changes for the better or the worse? [PARA] Let's begin by looking at the way tourism affects [P] peoples lives. For the individual traveller of course, the development of the tourist industry is an excellent thing. It has never been easier or cheaper to travel, and no part of the globe is beyond reach. Tourism improves the lives of many people because it brings jobs and [WW] prosper to regions that may otherwise [WF] had been very poor. But for some people, tourism is not a benefit. Those [WW] who's peace and quiet are ruined [PREP] for the arrival of the developers have no reason to praise the industry. [PARA] What about the effects of tourism [PREP] for wildlife? Well, there are advantages and disadvantages here, too. On the one hand, tourism has sometimes [SP] benefitted wildlife, especially in poor countries. If people have more money, they [WF] would protect the animals the tourists come to see, not hunt them. [PREP] In the other hand, it is true that tourists often damage habitats, even though this is usually unintentional. The pollution caused by tourism only makes the problem [WF] worst. [PARA] Is tourism, then, a blessing or a curse? I think it is both. The industry needs to take some responsible decisions in the future if the effects are to be beneficial rather than harmful.

12 Exam practice: Write an article discussing the pros and cons

You are going to write an article discussing pros and cons. Read the exam question and follow the instructions below.

Part 1

You **must** answer this question. Write your answer in **300–350 words** in an appropriate style.

Recently you saw a television programme where guests put forward arguments for and against keeping pets. Here are some of the things they said:

A pet is a status symbol for some people. They just want to impress their friends. Then they get tired of it and end up neglecting it.

People sometimes buy exotic pets like iguanas or baby alligators that are extremely hard to care for. They keep them in unsuitable conditions, so the animals have a very short lifespan.

It is good for children to keep pets. Learning to look after an animal teaches them to be patient and responsible.

Many old people find that pets are good company. Pets can help you to make friends too – new acquaintances have been formed by people who were out walking the dog in the park!

As a follow up, a magazine is planning to publish a series of articles on this topic and has asked readers to send in articles. You have decided to write an article putting forward arguments for and against keeping pets and referring to the quotes above.

Write your **article**.

- **Read the question**
  Underline all the points you need to cover in the exam question (including rubric and quotes).
- **Brainstorm the topic**
  Note down all your ideas. Then make a plan.
- **Think about format**
  Remember to set out your text as an article, with a title.
- **Think about style and tone**
  Remember to address your readers directly. Use rhetorical questions or similar devices.

9 Giving an opinion

1 Read the question

Read the exam question below carefully.

Part 1

You **must** answer this question. Write your answer in **300–350 words** in an appropriate style.

Last week, a television documentary explored ways in which we exploit animals. Read the extract from a review of the programme which was published in a weekly magazine.

> The programme started by questioning whether it is morally right to keep wild animals in zoos. We were shown footage of captive animals in highly unsuitable conditions. Not all zoos are this bad, it seems, but plenty are. The programme also considered whether animals should be used in laboratory tests. While the importance of medical research was acknowledged, the programme questioned the use of animals for testing cosmetics and perfumes. At the end of the programme we were left with the question: 'To what extent are we justified in exploiting animals in this way?'

You have been asked to write an article for the magazine, referring to the extract above and saying whether you think keeping animals in zoos or using them for research is ever justified and if it is, under what circumstances.

Write your **article**.

2 Think about your reader

Work with a partner. Look at the instructions (rubric) in the exam question again and answer the following questions.

1 Who is going to publish your article?
  - **a** a scientific journal
  - **b** a quality newspaper
  - **c** a weekly magazine

2 Who is going to read your article?
  - **a** biologists and other scientists
  - **b** the general public
  - **c** businesspeople

3 Should your article be
  - **a** formal and scientific?
  - **b** semi-formal/neutral?

4 Why are you writing the article?
  - **a** to review the programme
  - **b** to justify the making of the programme
  - **c** to give an opinion
  - **d** for some other reason

3 Identify the key points in the question

Work with a partner. Look at the extract in the exam question again and answer the following questions.

1 What was the subject of last week's TV programme?

2 Which two major topics must you consider? Underline them in the exam question. What else must you do in your article?

exam tip

If you are writing an article, always check what kind of publication you are writing for. While an article for a quality newspaper will probably need to be quite formal, magazine articles are often written in a neutral or semi-formal style.

4 Think about vocabulary

a Match the adjectives (1–9) with their opposites (a–i). (Sometimes more than one answer is possible.)

1	appalling	**a**	civilised
2	barbaric	**b**	defensible
3	cruel	**c**	essential
4	cramped	**d**	humane
5	inexcusable	**e**	painless
6	painful	**f**	spacious
7	pointless	**g**	superb
8	unnecessary	**h**	tame
9	wild	**i**	useful

b Complete the text with a suitable adjective from **a**. (Sometimes more than one answer is possible.)

I shall never forget my last visit to a zoo. The cages were so (1) .... that the animals barely had room to turn round. The keepers themselves were quite (2) .... and were doing their best to care for the animals but there was little they could do in such (3) .... conditions. It was the owner who was really to blame. He was greedy and (4) .... and totally unconcerned about what was going on around him. The way he way he treated his animals was absolutely (5) .... in my opinion.

c Match the words (1–6) with the words (a–f). Sometimes more than one answer is possible.

1	gain	**a**	a disease
2	do	**b**	a point of view/an opinion
3	test/make	**c**	an excuse
4	cure	**d**	drugs/medicine
5	make	**e**	experiments/research
6	justify	**f**	access

5 Brainstorm the topic

Work with a partner and answer the questions. Note down the best ideas.

1 Name five wild animals and five tame animals or pets. tiger panda, deer fox rabbit. polar beer, horse, cow, goat cat, dog.
2 Why are wild animals kept in captivity?
Make a list of reasons.
3 Have you been to a zoo recently? Describe it.
4 Do you think animals in captivity are always well-kept and happy?
Why/Why not?
5 What criticisms could you make about zoos?
6 Why do scientists use animals in research?
7 Do you think scientists are justified in using animals for research?
Why/Why not?
8 Should beauty products be tested on animals before they are sold in shops?
Why/Why not?

Factfile

Conditions vary greatly in zoos across the world. Some establishments pay scant heed to the requirements of the animals they have in captivity. Many animals show distress if kept in cages that are too small, or if they lack physical and/or mental stimulation. This distress often leads to repetitive behaviour, with animals pacing to and fro inside their cages.

The use of animals in research also arouses a great deal of passion. Many scientists argue it is essential to use laboratory animals for research to find cures for the world's major diseases. Opponents of these practices argue that most experiments involving animals are cruel and unnecessary, and that testing beauty products such as cosmetics and perfume on animals is immoral.

6 Make a plan

a Look at the following notes which one student has made. Tick (✓) the points you think he should include in his article. Put a cross (✗) against any points that are irrelevant or unimportant.

Notes
- conditions in some zoos
- keeping animals in zoos is wrong
- how captivity affects animals
- cruelty to pets
- using animals to test drugs okay?
- do we need to test beauty products on animals?
- how we use animals to help us, e.g. guide dogs

b Look at the plan below. The student has already completed most of the plan. Decide which notes he should put in Paragraph 3.

Plan

Paragraph 1: Should we keep animals in zoos/use them in research?

Paragraph 2: Why do we need zoos? How zoo animals suffer.

Paragraph 3: ....

Paragraph 4: Animals feel pain and many are intelligent. They suffer in any form of captivity.

tip

Make sure you give reasons for all your arguments. Don't make claims that you can't justify and avoid over-generalisations.

7 Read a model article

Read part of the article below and answer the following questions. Ignore the missing final paragraph for now.

1. Has the writer paragraphed his article clearly? Does he start a new paragraph for each new topic?
2. Underline the topic sentence in each paragraph.
3. Would a reader find the article interesting and well-argued?
4. Does the writer of the article address the reader directly? Find examples in the text.
5. Does the writer use rhetorical questions to make his article more direct?
6. Has the writer made his opinion clear to the reader all through the article?
7. Has he justified all his statements by giving examples or explanations? Find examples in the text.
8. Has the writer over-generalised in any of his points?
9. Has the writer forgotten any of the points he was asked to cover in the exam question?
10. Has the writer made any errors in grammar, spelling or punctuation?

Are we fair to animals?

We like to think that we live in a civilised society, but we are still capable of great cruelty. Consider the way we treat animals. We cage them, sometimes in appalling conditions, and we use them and even kill them in experiments. How can this be justified?

Conditions in zoos

Take a look at a zoo near you. Maybe you will be fortunate and find you live near a reputable zoo, where the animals are well cared for. This will not be the case for most of us, however. We are far more likely to find the sort of scenes shown in last week's television programme, with animals imprisoned in cramped cages in conditions unlike any they would experience in the wild. Like most wild animals that are kept in captivity they will show signs of distress. They may pace up and down their enclosures staring blindly ahead or sit listlessly in one corner of the cage. Few will reach even half the age they would in the wild, let alone breed in captivity. And why are they forced to endure these conditions? So that the owner of the zoo can make money, nothing more. Of course, not all zoos are like this, but as was shown in last week's programme, plenty are.

Animal research

Now consider the plight of those animals – mice, rabbits, dogs, cats and monkeys – that are kept in laboratories. Few of us have been inside one of these establishments; in fact, we would probably not be admitted if we tried. Nevertheless, we know enough about what goes on there to feel uneasy. Scientists argue that research is necessary if they are ever to find a cure for some of our most serious diseases – cancer, for example. Well, fair enough, this might justify some of the research involving animals. But surely we shouldn't be using animals to test products like cosmetics and shampoos? After all, we can't guarantee that a product will affect a human in the same way as an animal. And besides, do we really need more and more of these products? Surely we have got enough already!

The way forward

....

....

8 Think about your conclusion

Decide which of the paragraphs below (a–c) would make a good conclusion to this article. What is wrong with the others? Use this guide to help you.

A good conclusion to an article:

- is linked to the paragraph(s) before it.
- links back thematically to the first paragraph.
- contains a number of sentences that are well linked.
- may pose a question or make a clear statement.
- summarises the theme of the article and takes it on in some way.
- makes the article feel complete.

exam tip

The first and final paragraph of a text are often the most difficult to write, so leave yourself time in the exam to write a good introduction and conclusion.

a So are we justified in exploiting animals in the ways we have described? I believe not. Animals feel pain and emotion, and they suffer in captivity, whether in a zoo or laboratory. They deserve our respect and our consideration. As fellow creatures, they belong in their natural habitats, not in the prisons we make for them.

b To sum up, we should not keep animals in zoos or use them for experiments because it is cruel and barbaric.

c All in all, I don't believe using animals in laboratories is justifiable unless it is for serious medical research. Any other use should be made illegal and the penalties for breaking the law should be severe.

9 Think about language

Find words and phrases in the model article (including the conclusion) which mean the same as the following.

1 respected ....

2 to walk backwards and forwards, usually because you are worried or bored ....

3 in a tired and uninterested manner ....

4 to reproduce ....

5 to put up with ....

6 sad or unfortunate situation ....

7 allowed to enter ....

8 to promise ....

10 Compare two texts

a Read the essay below, which is on the same theme as the model article in **7**.

We like to think that we live in a civilised society, yet we are still capable of great cruelty. A good example of this can be found in the way we treat animals. We keep them caged up in conditions which are often appalling, and we even use them in laboratories to test new drugs, cosmetics and other pharmaceutical products. It is difficult to see how this treatment can be justified.

With regard to zoos, it must be accepted that a few, usually those in large cities, are concerned with the problem of animal welfare and do attempt to offer captive animals something like the surroundings they would enjoy in the wild. However, many other zoos are not so particular and the unfortunate animals in these places are confined in tiny cages which offer them little opportunity for movement or stimulation. A lot of animals show signs of distress and few reach even half the age they would in the wild. Sadly, these zoos are not concerned with issues such as animal conservation; they exist purely to satisfy the curiosity of the public.

Turning to the plight of animals in laboratories, it is even more difficult to find a justification for their treatment. It is very hard for the public to gain access to any of these establishments, which only increases the concern felt by many people about what goes on there. While there may be a strong argument for using animals to do research into cures for diseases like cancer, there seems little excuse for using them to test products like cosmetics and shampoos. There is no guarantee that these products will affect humans and animals in the same way, and besides, there is already a wide enough range of these products on sale in the shops.

To sum up, I believe that it is unacceptable to keep wild animals in zoos or to experiment on them, except in very few cases. We understand much more about animals now than we did in the past and this should prompt us to treat animals with respect. Failure to do so is, I believe, barbaric.

b Compare the essay in **a** with the model article. In what way is an article different to an essay? Put ticks (✓) in the correct column.

	Article	Essay
1 Sentences tend to be long and complex.		
2 The writer addresses the reader directly.		
3 The style is formal and impersonal.		
4 The tone is lively and conversational.		
5 There are a number of rhetorical questions.		
6 Passive forms are used quite frequently.		
7 There is a title.		
8 There may be sub-headings.		
9 Some verbs are in the imperative.		

exam tip

Read the exam question carefully and check what type of text you are being asked to write. An article is different from an essay or a letter, both in style and in format. Make sure you know the difference.

11 Think about language

Responding to opinions

The phrases in the box can be used to acknowledge and then dismiss opinions that differ from your own. Rewrite the following pairs of sentences, using appropriate phrases from the box.

Responding to opinions

While it might be argued that …,
the truth is that …

Although …, it must be remembered
that …

Some people claim that …
What they forget is that …

Despite claims that …,
it is a fact that …

It may be true that … but all too
often …

e.g. Animals in zoos are sometimes well looked after. All too often, they are not.
It may be true that animals in zoos are sometimes well looked after, but all too often, they are not.

1 Some experiments on animals are done for medical reasons. In the majority of cases, they are not.

………………………………………………………………………………………

2 We do not credit animals with having emotions. They do experience fear and stress.

………………………………………………………………………………………

3 Scientists are not deliberately cruel to animals. They do sometimes cause them pain and discomfort.

………………………………………………………………………………………

4 Some animals seem to adapt quite happily to living in cages. Most wild animals suffer if kept in captivity.

………………………………………………………………………………………

12 Exam practice: Write an article giving an opinion

You are going to write an article giving an opinion. Read the exam question and follow the instructions below.

Part 1

You **must** answer this question. Write your answer in **300–350 words** in an appropriate style.

The extract below comes from a lecture you heard recently on reasons for becoming a vegetarian. You have decided to write an article on the subject for a weekly magazine referring to the points raised in the extract and giving your own views.

> There are more reasons than ever to become a vegetarian. Pictures of battery hens and other horrors have revealed the cruelty involved in intensive farming. These practices have not improved the quality of our food – they have made it worse. Think, for example, of Bovine Spongiform Encephalitis (BSE), or Mad Cow Disease, which can spread from cattle to humans with disastrous consequences. There have been worries about the other meat we buy too, such as chicken and veal. As well as all the food scares, doctors warn us that eating too much meat is bad for our health. It is hardly surprising that thinking people are weighing up the pros and cons of eating meat and turning vegetarian.

Write your **article**.

- **Read the question**
  Underline all the points you need to cover in the exam question. Remember to include points in the instructions (rubric) as well as those in the input text(s).
- **Think about style, tone and format**
  Remember how an article differs from other kinds of text.
- **Make a plan**
  Make sure you plan what you are going to say *before* you start to write.
- **Think about paragraphing**
  Start a new paragraph for each new topic. Link your paragraphs. Write a topic sentence for each paragraph.
- **Think about your arguments**
  Always justify your claims by giving an example or an explanation. Don't over-generalise.
- **Think about your introduction and conclusion**
  Allow yourself enough time to write a good introduction and conclusion.

10 Giving an opinion

1 Read the question

Read the exam question below carefully.

Part 1

You **must** answer this question. Write your answer in **300–350 words** in an appropriate style.

You recently attended a lecture on the causes of delinquency and bad behaviour in young people. Among other things, the speaker said:

'Evidence shows that young people are increasingly likely to get into trouble with the authorities for some reason or another. They may be guilty of minor misdemeanours such as rowdy behaviour in public or vandalism, or of more serious offences, such as drug taking and theft. Why do some young people flout authority and get into trouble and what should be done to prevent this? Some experts argue that parents need to be much stricter with their offspring. Others relate behaviour problems to the pressures young people face in today's world. Many experts agree that scenes of crime or violence on film and television may lead young people astray, as may the wrong kind of peer pressure.'

As a follow up, your course tutor has asked you to write an essay commenting on the extract above and examining the reasons why some young people behave badly. You should also give your opinion as to whether parents should be stricter with their children.

Write your **essay**.

exam information

Essays may occur in both parts of the Writing Paper. You will be expected to produce a fairly formal piece of writing which is well-structured and clear.

2 Think about your reader

Work with a partner. Look at the exam question again and answer the following questions.

1 What kind of text are you asked to write?

2 Who is going to read your text?

3 What style of language will your reader expect?
- **a** formal
- **b** quite informal
- **c** colloquial

4 What format do you need to use?
- **a** letter format
- **b** article format
- **c** paragraphed text with no specific format

5 For what purpose are you writing?
To give an opinion? To complain?
To give reasons? For some other reason?

3 Identify the key points in the question

Look at the exam question again and answer the following questions.

1 What was the subject of the lecture you recently attended?

2 What kinds of misbehaviour are young people sometimes guilty of, according to the speaker?

3 Name four possible reasons for bad behaviour in young people which are alluded to by the speaker.

4 What are the *three* main things you must do in your essay? Underline them.

4 Brainstorm the topic

Work with a partner and answer the questions. Note down the best ideas.

1 Do you agree that some young people behave badly these days? Give examples.

2 Do you think parents are stricter or more lenient than they used to be? In what ways?

3 Do you think any of the following influence young people's behaviour? If so, how?
- films and television
- peer pressure
- increased spending power

4 Do you think young people have more freedom now than in the past? If so, in what ways? Is this a good thing?

5 Do you think young people are affected if both their parents go out to work full-time? If so, how?

6 What kinds of stresses and temptations do young people face these days?

7 Do you think bad behaviour is caused by a lack of discipline? What other causes are there?

exam tip

It isn't always easy to think of arguments for a discursive essay under exam conditions but it gets easier with practice. Try looking at recent exam questions and brainstorming ideas on paper. Give yourself a time limit, say five minutes. It will save a lot of panic on the day of the exam!

5 Make a plan

a Look at the exam question again and also at the notes you brainstormed. Group related ideas together and decide where to put them on the plan below. (You can add paragraphs if necessary.)

b Write a topic sentence for each paragraph.

Paragraph 1
Topic: *Introduction: Most young people are well behaved but some are not. Why?*
Topic sentence: *While most young people these days are well-behaved, it is a fact that a minority behave very badly.*

Paragraph 2
Topic: ....
Topic sentence: ....

Paragraph 3
Topic: ....
Topic sentence: ....

Paragraph 4
Topic: ....
Topic sentence: ....

tip

Remember to make a plan *before* you start to write. This is especially important in discursive essays. You need to put forward a clear, logical argument that the reader can follow easily.

6 Think about vocabulary

a Write the words in the box in a suitable category. Some words may belong to more than one category.

authoritarian delinquent discipline disobedient easy-going harsh hooligan lenient neglect rebel rebellious reprimand scold strict tolerance undisciplined vandal well behaved

Adjectives that describe parents: ....
Adjectives that describe young people: ....
People: ....
Abstract nouns: ....
Verbs: ....

b Complete the following paragraph with words from **a**. Make any necessary changes. (Sometimes more than one answer is possible.)

In the past, parents tended to be very strict but now they are far more (1) .... Critics argue that parents should exercise more (2) .... They claim that if parents and teachers were (3) ...., young people would be less (4) .... and maybe we would have fewer football (5) .... and (6) .... in our society. But are the critics right? After all, it is the nature of young people to be (7) .... and to challenge those in authority over them from time to time.

7 Think about your introduction

a The first paragraph of a text often begins with a topic sentence, which is explained or illustrated in the sentences that follow. Look at the list of opening phrases below. They are often used at the beginning of topic sentences.

It is often said that ...
It is often argued that ...
It is a fact that ...
Over the past few years, it seems that ...
Recently we have all become concerned that ...
In the past, people ..., but now ...
These days, it seems that ...
Nowadays, we are becoming aware of the fact that ...

b Write the first paragraph of your essay, using one of the phrases above.

8 Think about language

Giving opinions

a Your essay should be written in a formal style. Tick (✓) the phrases below that are appropriate for a formal essay. Put a cross (✗) against those that are inappropriate.

1 I firmly believe that ...
2 It's rubbish to say that ...
3 It's stupid to believe that ...
4 It would seem to me that ...
5 You have to be mad to believe that ...
6 I tend to think that ...
7 Believe me, ...
8 I am inclined to believe that ...

b The phrases in the box below are often used to give personal opinions. Can you add any more examples?

I believe/do not believe that ... (because) ...
Personally, I feel that ... (as) ...
It seems to me that ... This is because ...
I would argue that ...
I feel strongly that ...
I am convinced that ...
I am (greatly) in favour of/against ...
I am (completely) opposed to ...

9 Think about style

In discursive writing, especially essays, it is important not to make over-generalisations, as these are inaccurate and also tend to alienate the reader. Compare the phrases in each pair below. Say which phrase in each pair will lead to an over-generalisation and which will qualify a statement and make it more cautious.

1 **a** Everybody knows that ...
b Many people believe that ...

2 **a** People tend to ...
b People always ...

3 **a** People never ...
b People often ...

4 **a** Not everybody believes that ...
b Nobody believes that ...

5 **a** All young people are ...
b The majority of young people are ...

6 **a** Young people get into trouble because ...
b Young people may get into trouble because ....

10 Read a model essay

Read the model essay below and use this checklist to decide if it is a good essay.

1. Has the writer answered the exam question in full?
2. Has she included anything that is irrelevant?
3. Has she used the correct style and format for an essay?
4. Has she divided her essay into clear, well developed paragraphs?
5. Are her ideas clear and easy to follow?
6. Does she follow up each of her arguments by giving an example or an explanation?
7. Has she made any over-generalisations?
8. Has she written a well-developed introduction and conclusion?

While it is a fact that most young people these days are well behaved, it is also true that a minority behave very badly. Over the past few years, it seems that incidents of vandalism and delinquency have mushroomed. There are examples of this everywhere – at football matches, in parks and on street corners. Our newspapers are full of reports about juveniles beyond parental control, who have plunged into the seamy world of drugs or crime. So what are the causes?

In my opinion, there are a number of reasons why some young people misbehave. In the first place, as was stated in the lecture, they face many more challenges than in the past. At school, the pressure to pass exams, to master technology, and to find a job is becoming ever greater. At home, children can no longer rely on their parents to be there to talk over their problems and worries with them. Today's mothers and fathers are busy following their career paths, and many no longer have the energy to spend quality time with their offspring.

Another cause of bad behaviour may be found in the sort of television programmes and films young people watch. Many films contain bad language or violence, and, as our lecturer pointed out, impressionable young people may copy this. Peer pressure, it is also true, may constitute a formidable force in many youngsters' lives and the temptation to be 'one of the gang' has led many children astray. This problem is greater when there is not enough for young people to do. Boredom is a major cause of delinquency, so it is important to provide sufficient facilities for young people, such as clubs and sports centres.

People often say that there has been a breakdown in discipline in the home and that parents should be stricter. However, I do not believe this is always the cause of bad behaviour. As I see it, young people need support and guidance from parents and other adults in their lives, rather than an authoritarian approach.

To sum up, there are many reasons why young people misbehave. Although lack of discipline may play a part, it is not the main factor. Adults need to understand the pressures young people face and to provide them with the love, support and guidance they need, if they are to solve the problem of bad behaviour.

11 Think about connectors

The words and phrases in the box below are used to show contrast. Look back at the model essay and find examples of these.

whereas	On the other hand, ...
although	however
even though	nevertheless
in spite of/despite	nonetheless
while	yet
On the one hand, ... (but)	

12 Exam practice: Write an essay giving an opinion

You are going to write an essay giving an opinion. Read the exam question and follow the instructions below.

Part 1

You **must** answer this question. Write your answer in **300–350 words** in an appropriate style.

Recently, you watched a television programme about crime punishment. This is what one of the speakers said:

'Recent crime figures make grim reading. As our prisons grow more crowded, we need to think more about what makes an individual turn to crime and whether there is more society can do to prevent this. It appears that the roots of crime are often found in poverty and unemployment. Lack of education and the absence of a firm moral upbringing are major factors too. Along with a consideration of the causes of crime, we need to think about how we deal with criminals. Should sentencing be harsher or more lenient? Should we concentrate on reforming prisoners or should our main concern be punishment?'

Your course tutor has now asked you to write an essay, referring to the statement above and examining the causes of crime and the way criminals are punished in your country. In your essay, you should say whether you think society is tough enough on criminals.

Write your **essay**.

- **Read the question**
  Remember to underline the issues you must cover in the exam question.
- **Brainstorm the topic**
  Note down ideas. Then go through them and cross out those that are irrelevant or less important.
- **Make a paragraph plan**
  Don't try to include too many points in your essay. Stick to a few arguments but make sure you develop them fully.
- **Think about style**
  Back up your statements with examples or explanations. Don't over-generalise.
- **Link your text**
  Use connectors where appropriate to link sentences and paragraphs together.
- **Think about your introduction and conclusion**
  Remember that these are often the most difficult part of your task. Leave yourself plenty of time to think about them.

11 Presenting both sides of an argument

1 Read the question

Read the exam question below carefully.

Part 1

You **must** answer this question. Write your answer in **300–350 words** in an appropriate style.

Recently, you and your fellow students attended a lecture on genetic engineering, given by a well-known scientist. Below is a quotation from her talk. The lecture provoked a great deal of interest and consequently, the editors of your school newspaper have decided to hold an essay-writing competition on the subject and have invited submissions. Write an essay referring to the quotation and saying whether, in your view, the advantages of genetic engineering outweigh the risks.

'The genes we inherit from our parents govern not only our physical appearance, such as what colour eyes we have, but also influence our behaviour. Scientists have now learnt how to alter the genes of plants, animals and even humans. This 'genetic engineering' can be used to produce disease-resistant crops and healthier, larger farm animals. It can be used to treat human diseases. Scientists can even clone animals and may one day clone a human being. The problem is that genetic engineering interferes with the natural processes of evolution. The long-term effects of what we are doing are unknown, and could be disastrous. Is it worth the risk?'

Write your **essay**.

exam tip

Remember that in Part 1 of the Writing Paper you must cover *all* the points you are asked for, otherwise you will lose marks. Read the instructions and the input material carefully and underline all the important points.

2 Think about your reader

Work with a partner. Look at the instructions (rubric) in the exam question again and answer the following questions.

1. What have you attended? What was it about?
2. Where does the extract come from?
3. What sort of text have you been asked to write?
4. Who is going to read your text?
5. For what purpose are you writing? To give your opinion? To oppose the idea of genetic engineering? To defend genetic engineering? To examine the advantages and the risks? For some other reason?

3 Think about register

Work with a partner. Look at the instructions (rubric) in the exam question again and answer the following questions.

1 Who are you writing your text for?
- **a** your course tutor
- **b** your fellow students
- **c** the readers of a scientific journal
- **d** people who like science fiction stories

2 What style should you use?
- **a** formal
- **b** informal

4 Identify the key points in the question

Work with a partner. Look at the extract in the exam question again and answer the following questions.

1. Where do we get our genes from? What do genes do?
2. What can scientists now do to genes?
3. What effect can genetic engineering have on plants and animals? On humans?
4. What are 'clones'? Can scientists clone animals? What about humans?
5. What is the problem with genetic engineering?

5 Think about vocabulary

a Match the words and phrases (1–10) with their definitions (a–j).

1 cell
2 gene
3 species
4 mutation
5 cloning
6 experiment
7 genetic engineering
8 inherited characteristics
9 gene therapy
10 evolution

- **a** the process by which plants and animals gradually develop from simpler to more complicated forms
- **b** making an exact copy of a plant or animal by taking a cell from it and developing it artificially
- **c** a thorough test using scientific methods
- **d** a small part of the material inside the nucleus of a cell that controls the development of the qualities that have been passed on to a living thing from its parents
- **e** a way of treating certain diseases by adding to the body a gene it does not have
- **f** the smallest part of a living thing that can exist independently
- **g** the science of changing the genetic structure of an animal, plant or human to affect the way it develops
- **h** a change in the genetic structure of an animal or plant
- **i** a group of animals or plants which can breed together to produce young plants or animals of the same kind
- **j** special, recognisable qualities (e.g. colour of eyes) passed on by parents, grandparents, etc.

11 Presenting both sides of an argument

b Write the words in the box in the correct category. Some of the words are both nouns and verbs.

abnormal alarmist alter amazing avoid ban behaviour breakthrough breed characteristic clone consumer create crop design develop discover ensure evolution genetic govern harm immune inherit life-threatening mutate pest pesticide profitable reassure research safety selection species technique therapy unacceptable worrying

Verbs: ....

....

Nouns: ....

....

Adjectives: ....

....

c Complete the factfile with words and phrases from **a** or **b**. Make any necessary changes. The first letter(s) of each answer has been provided.

Factfile

Genetic engineering

- The genes you have i.................................. from your parents influence many aspects of your physical appearance and your b.................................. . Now scientists have learnt how to alter these genes and radically change the natural process of evolution.
- Scientists can use genetic e.................................. to grow crops which can tolerate drought or are i.................................. to disease or insects. This means there is more food for people to eat – and makes farmers' profits larger!
- Fruit and vegetables can be genetically modified to make them stay ripe longer without rotting.
- Scientists can b.................................. offspring from animals like cows which will give more milk or better meat.
- Scientists can even c.................................. animals to produce duplicates. This t.................................. could be used to save some wild animals from extinction.
- It is not yet known how g..................................-engineered plants and animals may affect the balance of nature.
- Gene th.................................. can be used to treat some diseases in humans. At the moment, people with genetic diseases may pass these on to their children. Soon it may be possible for doctors to cure genetic disease in an embryo.
- In the future, scientists may be able to supply everyone with a 'gene profile'. Then you will know about all the diseases you might have inherited from your parents and that you may develop in the future.
- In theory, genetics could be used to change human beings mentally and physically. Scientists could try to d.................................. the 'perfect' human, without any physical or mental defects and with specific features such as a particular colour of eyes.

6 Brainstorm the topic

Work with a partner. Look at the pictures and statements and answer the questions. Make notes on your answers.

1 How can genetically-engineered plants help farmers? Why would the technique be very useful in developing countries?

2 Genetically-engineered food is already on sale in the shops, but no experiments have yet been done to test its effect on humans. Do you think it is a good idea to sell the food without these tests? Why?/Why not?

3 In the film *Jurassic Park*, scientists recreated animals that were extinct from a small amount of DNA. Scientists have already cloned animals such as sheep. They could clone endangered species, like tigers or gorillas. Would this be a good idea? Why?/Why not?

4 Experiments in genetic engineering are often carried out on animals and inevitably involve some suffering on the part of the animal. Should we treat animals in this way?

5 Should scientists use gene therapy to correct abnormal genes in people with life-threatening inherited illnesses, like cystic fibrosis?

6 What might your employer or your life insurance company do if they knew you would probably develop a serious illness in the future? Would *you* want to know if you were probably going to develop an incurable disease later in life? Why?/Why not?

7 In the future, scientists may be able to 'correct' the genes that govern 'anti-social' behaviour, like aggression. Should governments ask them to do this? What are the dangers?

8 Should we, as individuals, be able to change our genes if we don't like the way we are? Why?/Why not?

9 Do you think there is a chance that scientists could ever clone human beings? Why might scientists/governments want to do this? Do you think it would be wrong? Why?/Why not?

10 How far should we let scientists go with genetic engineering? Is what they are doing acceptable socially and morally? Should there be any limits or safeguards?

7 Make a plan

a Organise the notes you have brainstormed under the headings below.

Advantages	Risks
....	....
....	....

b Look at the two possible essay outlines below. Work with a partner and discuss which would be best to use for this essay and why.

A

- introduction
- one or more paragraphs dealing with the advantages
- one or more paragraphs dealing with the risks
- conclusion

B

- introduction
- one or more paragraphs dealing with the first set of advantages and risks
- one or more paragraphs dealing with the second set of advantages and risks
- conclusion

8 Think about connectors

Look at the phrases below that can be used to state, weigh up or summarise two sides of an argument. Can you add any more?

Weighing up and stating arguments

One of the most significant advantages/disadvantages of … is …

One of the main risks in … is …

It is important to remember that …

While it is true that …, it must not be forgotten that …

Although it could be argued that …, it is also a fact that …

Summarising arguments

All in all, I tend to the view that …

On balance, I think that …

Taking everything into consideration, I would say that …

9 Read a model essay

Read the model essay below.

Over the past decades, scientists have made major discoveries in genetic engineering. *They* can now alter the genes of any living thing and may soon be able to design 'perfect' plants, animals and even human beings. There is no doubt that genetic engineering can benefit humankind, but things could also go very wrong.

One of the greatest benefits of genetic engineering could be in agriculture. Farmers can now grow crops engineered to be resistant to drought and disease and to natural pests. *This* could solve some of the major problems facing farmers in developing countries and provide food for many more starving people. Yet there are risks. If we destroy pests such as insects, what will happen to the birds and animals that usually feed on *them*? There is also concern about the effect on the health of human beings who eat this modified food.

Another advantage lies in the field of medicine. Gene therapy may soon allow doctors to cure babies with inherited diseases, even before *they* are born. Indeed, it may soon be possible for all of us to have a 'gene profile', so we can see if we are likely to develop a fatal disease, like cancer, as we grow older. We can then try to reduce the risk, for example by not smoking cigarettes. *This* is good but, on the other hand, do we really want to know that we are going to develop a fatal illness? It is, moreover, worrying to think how some insurance companies and employers might use *this information* against the interests of the individual.

Some scientists claim that in the future they will be able to design the perfect human being and *this* might sound like yet another advantage at first. Governments could make sure that there were no longer people who were 'anti-social' or 'abnormal'. Yet the idea that anyone can judge what is 'normal' and 'acceptable' in human beings, and eliminate characteristics they disapprove of, is actually very frightening. Add to *that* the possibility of cloning human beings, as has been done with animals, and we can see that the risks of *this new science* are very great.

(missing conclusion)

10 Think about your conclusion

Read the three possible conclusions (a–c) to the model essay above. Decide which one is best and why.

a Genetic engineering has advantages, but it also has risks, so scientists should follow the guidelines set down for them.

b On balance, it would seem that genetic engineering offers benefits, but also tremendous risks. We need to be very sure that guidelines set down are rigorously followed by scientists. Only if the knowledge we have is used maturely and responsibly will it be of benefit to mankind, rather than a disaster.

c I could say a lot more about the advantages and dangers of genetic engineering but I have not got enough time now. The possibilities are endless.

11 Think about paragraphing

a Look back at the model essay on p.76. Write a brief summary of each paragraph in the spaces below.

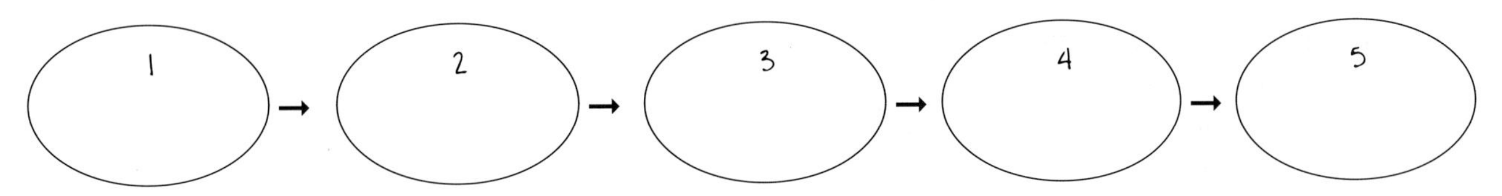

b Underline the topic sentence in each of the paragraphs.

c The words in *italics* in the model essay help to link the text together. Highlight the words or information they refer back to in the text.

12 Exam practice: Write an essay presenting both sides of an argument

You are going to write an essay presenting both sides of an argument. Read the exam question and follow the instructions below.

Part 1

You **must** answer this question. Write your answer in **300–350 words** in an appropriate style.

Recently, you and your fellow students attended a public lecture on nuclear power. Below is a quotation from the talk. Now your course tutor has asked you to write an essay, outlining the pros and cons of using nuclear power and commenting on the issues raised in the talk.

'Experts tell us that in about fifty years from now, the world's oil resources may finally be exhausted. The answer to the world's energy problems could lie in the development of more nuclear power stations. Nuclear power is a very clean form of energy and does not cause the high levels of environmental pollution that conventional power stations do. However, as critics are quick to point out, nuclear power stations carry their own dangers. Many stations now in operation are notoriously unsafe and those unfortunate enough to live nearby live in dread of the next accident. Explosions, such as the one at the nuclear power plant in Chernobyl some years ago, can contaminate large areas with radioactive fallout and kill thousands of people. So should we build more nuclear power stations or not?'

Write your **essay**.

- **Read the question**
  Underline all the points you have to cover in the exam question.
- **Brainstorm the topic**
  Make notes before you start to write.
- **Make a plan**
  Organise your ideas for and against into separate paragraphs.
- **Edit your text**
  Always leave time to check your grammar, spelling and punctuation.

12 Outlining problems and offering a solution

1 Read the question

Read the exam question below carefully.

Part 1

You **must** answer this question. Write your answer in **300–350 words** in an appropriate style.

The extract below is part of a magazine article on stress, which you read in class recently. Your course tutor has now asked you to write an essay, examining some of the causes of stress, and outlining some strategies to cope with the problem. In your essay you should respond to the questions posed in the article, and say whether you think life today is more stressful than it was in the past.

Nowadays, doctors' waiting rooms are packed with patients complaining of stress and stress-related ailments. But what is it about modern life that makes it so stressful? Is it the pace of change that is causing us such anxiety? Or is stress born of our doubts about traditional beliefs, religious or otherwise, which were the props of human existence in the past? Are we really living under more pressure than our forebears? And what can we do to allay the worst effects of this most modern condition?

Write your **essay**.

2 Think about your reader

Work with a partner. Look at the instructions (rubric) in the exam question again and answer the following questions.

1 Where does the extract come from?

2 What kind of text have you been asked to write?

3 For what purpose are you writing the text?

4 Who are you writing for?

5 Will your reader expect your style to be
   a chatty and informal?
   b serious and informative?

3 Identify the key points in the question

Look at the extract in the exam question again and answer the following questions.

1 What is stress and why is it a problem?

2 What are some of the possible causes of stress?

3 Why might our lives be more stressful than those of our forebears?

4 You are asked to do *four* things in your essay. What are they? Underline them in the exam question.

Factfile

When animals experience stress, it is usually because they are faced with a physical threat or danger. In such situations, their adrenal glands produce the hormone adrenalin, which causes the heart to beat faster, the muscles to tense, and blood pressure to increase. This is commonly known as the 'flight or fight' response because it helps the animal either to run away to save itself or to stay and fight. The response has great survival value, as an animal that is not physically ready for 'flight or fight' is likely soon to be a dead animal! When the situation is resolved, the body returns to its normal state. Human beings also have the 'flight or fight' response, which enabled our forebears to cope with, and survive, the dangers they faced.

Modern life involves stresses that are more likely to be psychological rather than physical but our bodies continue to react in the same way; we have not evolved any new responses or mechanisms to deal with our changed circumstances. We tense up but have no way to relieve the tension. The result may be chronic stress, one of the most widespread problems of modern life, and one that puts our health – physical and mental – at risk.

People who suffer from chronic stress become overwhelmed by the accumulation of everyday anxieties caused by overwork, losing a job and so on. Stress is probably a greater problem now than in former times because the pace of change is so fast. Many traditional beliefs have been brought into question, and some people feel lost in a sea of doubt. In many countries, family ties have broken down, so the individual may have less emotional support than in the past.

While nobody can escape feelings of stress, there are many ways to counter its effects. Effective strategies include taking exercise, learning to relax, or adopting some of the many natural remedies which allay the worst effects of stress.

4 Think about vocabulary

a Complete the following sentences with words from the box.

allay evolved frenetic niggling relief strategies ties uproot

1. We need to learn new .... to cope with the effects of stress.
2. Most of us have little .... worries that lurk at the back of our minds.
3. Our ancestors lived in a world that was not so .... as ours.
4. Exercise provides .... because it allows you to let off steam.
5. Animals have .... physical and behavioural mechanisms to deal with danger.
6. Sandra was petrified of going into hospital, but I managed to .... most of her fears by explaining what was going to happen.
7. During a war, families often have to ....themselves and move away from the war zone.
8. In the past, people had close family ...., but these bonds have become looser in modern societies.

b Match the adjectives (1–6) that collocate with the nouns (a–f).

1 deep	**a** support
2 chronic	**b** fingers
3 trembling	**c** palms
4 irrational	**d** breathing
5 sweaty	**e** stress
6 emotional	**f** fears

c Complete the following sentences with phrases from **b**.

1 Her .... prevented her from holding the paper still.

2 Luckily, I have a big family and they give me .... in times of crisis.

3 I had such .... I had to keep wiping my hands on my trousers.

4 Children frequently become prey to ...., such as imagining there are ghosts behind the curtains.

5 The yoga teacher talked to us about the importance of .... and relaxation.

6 If you suffer from ...., you feel anxious all the time.

5 Brainstorm the topic

Work with a partner and answer the questions. Note down the best ideas.

1 What are some of the major causes of stress? What are some of the physical manifestations of stress? Is stress good for you? Why/Why not?

2 What makes *you* feel stressed?

3 Do you think life this century is more stressful than it was in the past? Why/Why not?

4 What can people do to reduce their stress levels? Do you know of any really good stress relievers? What do you personally find useful?

6 Make a plan

a Look at the exam question again and also at the notes you brainstormed. Group related ideas together and decide where to put them on the plan below. You can add paragraphs if necessary.

Plan

Paragraph 1
Introduction: ....

Paragraph 2
....

Paragraph 3
....

Paragraph 4
....

Paragraph 5
....

exam tip

Remember that there is a word limit in the exam. Select your best ideas and make sure you develop each of them appropriately.

7 Read a model essay

a Read the model essay below.

Most of us feel stressed at some time in our lives. Anyone who has sat for a crucial examination or given a speech in public will recognise the symptoms: sweaty palms, a pounding heart, an inability to concentrate. Stress is a reaction to a danger, real or perceived and the strength of this reaction differs from person to person.

Stress is nothing new. Our primitive ancestors experienced stress when they were faced by a physical threat – an attack by wild animals, for example. They had two choices: to run away or to fight. After the physical activity required for either, their bodies would have returned to a normal, relaxed state.

The world has changed, however, and the sort of stress we experience nowadays is mental rather than physical. Unlike our ancestors, we live in a world which often seems unpredictable and uncontrollable, and in which the old certainties seem to have disappeared. In this technological maelstrom, we feel pushed and pulled in all directions. The pressures can be intense, yet many people can no longer rely on their family for emotional support, as they could in the past. Those who work increasingly long hours, stuck at a desk or in front of a computer, have little time to work off the stress caused by niggling worries or petty irritations.

Fortunately, there are strategies we can adopt to mitigate or even dispel the effects of stress. Sport is an excellent stress reliever as it allows you to work off feelings of anxiety through physical activity. Other stress relievers involve using the creative part of your brain – playing an instrument for example, or painting – and distracting your mind from negative thoughts. Yoga and meditation relieve stress as they involve deep relaxation, as do natural therapies such as aromatherapy.
(missing conclusion)

b Now read the two concluding paragraphs, a and b, below. Which paragraph would make a good conclusion? Give *two* reasons for your choice.

a The world today is changing and developing at such a rapid pace that it is bound to leave us feeling stressed and anxious. However, by learning to recognise the symptoms of stress we can allay its worst effects and learn to cope, just as our ancestors did in very different conditions in the past.

b If we confront stressful situations in the ways I have described, we might be able to solve some of these problems.

c Look back at the model essay in **a**. Then go through this list and tick the appropriate column. Does the essay constitute a good answer to the question?

1	Does the essay cover all the points asked for in the exam question?	Yes ☐	No ☐
2	Does the essay pay insufficient attention to any of the points to be covered?	Yes ☐	No ☐
3	Is the essay divided into logical, well-developed paragraphs?	Yes ☐	No ☐
4	Is the introduction too short/long?	Yes ☐	No ☐
5	Is the vocabulary very basic?	Yes ☐	No ☐
6	Does the writer use a range of complex structures correctly?	Yes ☐	No ☐
7	Does the writer make a lot of over-generalisations?	Yes ☐	No ☐
8	Does the writer back up statements with examples and explanations?	Yes ☐	No ☐
9	Does the writer make many basic grammatical errors?	Yes ☐	No ☐
10	Is the essay too short?	Yes ☐	No ☐

d Write a brief summary of each paragraph of the model essay in the boxes below.

1 → 2 → 3 → 4 → 5

e Has the writer included a topic sentence in each of his paragraphs? Underline them.

exam tip

Make sure your essay is the right length. If you become familiar with the length, you will not need to waste time counting the exact number of words in the exam.

8 Think about grammar

Relative clauses

Join the sentences below using a relative clause.

1 We live in a world. It often seems unpredictable and uncontrollable.

....

2 People lack emotional support in times of crisis. These people have been forced to uproot themselves to search for work.

....

3 Stress is a reaction to a threat. The threat can be real or perceived.

....

4 There are recognisable symptoms of stress. We have all experienced them.

....

5 Some people can become seriously ill. These people fail to cope with stress.

....

6 Stress relievers are activities. They relieve the effects of stress.

....

9 Think about language

The phrases listed below are often used in this type of essay. Can you find any of the phrases in the model essay? If so, underline them.

Outlining a situation/problem
Nowadays, it seems that …
Anyone who has … will know that …
Over recent years people have become concerned that …

Explaining
There are a number of reasons for this.
One of the causes of … is …
This is largely due to …
This has led to/caused …
This means that …

Suggesting solutions
Fortunately, there are ways in which we can solve this problem.
There are many ways in which we could …
It is essential that we …
The most obvious solution is to …
If we …, we will be able to …

10 Exam practice: Write an essay outlining problems and offering a solution

You are going to write an essay outlining problems and offering a solution. Read the exam question and follow the instructions below.

Part 1

You **must** answer this question. Write your answer in **300–350 words** in an appropriate style.

The extract below is part of a magazine article you read in class recently. Your course tutor has now asked you to write an essay, outlining the problems caused by the intrusion of the media into people's lives and the effect this has on the individual. In your essay you should refer to the article and suggest possible solutions to the problem.

> The privacy of the individual is being invaded as never before. It seems there is nothing that our tabloid newspapers or more sensational magazines will not print in their bid to win the circulation war. Celebrities are hounded through the streets. The paparazzi lurk behind bushes or break into private residences, eager to take that one revealing shot that will make the pages of the Sunday paper. The private lives of politicians, film stars, and models are offered up to the public gaze and their children and families are stalked as they go about their everyday lives. Surely we could do more to prevent this unwarranted intrusion into people's lives.

Write your **essay**.

- **Brainstorm the topic**
  Underline the points you need to cover in the exam question. Then brainstorm ideas and select the best ones.
- **Make a plan**
  Make a paragraph plan so that your essay is well-organised and logical.
- **Think about paragraphing**
  Start a new paragraph for each fresh topic. Develop each idea and explain or illustrate any statements or arguments you make.
- **Think about your introduction and conclusion**
  Make sure these are well-developed and of interest to the reader.

13 Writing a proposal (1)

1 Read the question

Read the exam question below carefully.

Part 2

Write your answer in **300–350 words** in an appropriate style.

The tourist office you work for wants to help boost the local economy by attracting more visitors to your area, both from within your own country and from abroad. The office manager has asked you to write a proposal on ways to attract more tourists and to outline some ideas on how to improve tourist amenities in the area.

Write your **proposal**.

exam information

Proposals may occur in both parts of the Writing Paper. A proposal is very similar in format to a report. However, while a report generally focuses on a past or present situation, a proposal usually focuses on the future and makes recommendations for future action.

2 Think about your reader

Work with a partner. Look at the exam question again and answer the following questions.

1 Who has asked you to write this proposal?
  a a colleague
  b a friend
  c your superior

2 Should your language be
  a formal?
  b informal?

3 For what purpose are you writing the proposal? To earn a larger salary? To make suggestions? To recommend something? To put forward ideas? For some other reason?

3 Think about register

a Study the list below. Tick (✓) the features you would expect to find in a formal proposal.

- impersonal statements
- passive forms
- idiomatic language
- complex sentences
- slang
- a tentative, diplomatic style
- a large number of phrasal verbs
- sophisticated vocabulary, used with precision
- a conversational style

b Tick (✓) the more formal option in the pairs of sentences below.

1 **a** The aim of this proposal is to put forward some ideas on how to attract visitors to our town.
b Here are some ideas I have noted down on attracting visitors to our town.

2 **a** Let's build a visitor centre.
b I propose we build a visitor centre.

3 **a** Kids are put off coming to our town because there is nowhere to stay.
b Younger visitors are discouraged from coming to our town because of the shortage of accommodation.

4 **a** A 'park and ride' system has been adopted in many cities.
b They have got a 'park and ride' system in lots of cities.

5 **a** Our area has much to offer.
b There is lots to do in our area.

6 **a** I propose that we allocate a portion of our annual budget to advertising.
b Why don't we spend some of our money every year on advertising?

4 Identify the key points in the question

Work with a partner. Look at the exam question again and answer the following questions.

1 Who do you work for?

2 Which *two* groups of tourists do you want to attract to your area?

3 According to the exam question, how will this increase in tourism benefit the area?

4 What does the manager want to hear from you regarding amenities?

5 Underline all the issues you have to cover in your proposal, then complete the list below.

- *How to attract tourists* (a) *from our own country and* (b) ....
- ....
- ....

13 Writing a proposal (1)

5 Brainstorm the topic

Work with a partner and answer the questions. Note down the best ideas.

1 Imagine you want to attract more visitors to your town. What amenities in your area do you think are important to tourists?
Think about car parks, shops, leisure centres, visitor centres, parks, cinemas, theatres etc. Which of these should be improved? How?

2 How do you think your town could attract more visitors (a) from abroad and (b) from your own country? Should you offer special attractions? Build more amenities, e.g. for young people? Advertise? Do something else?

tip

It is much easier to brainstorm ideas if you think of a concrete example. In this case, think of an area you know *personally* and then work out how to attract more tourists there.

6 Make a plan

Look at one student's plan. Organise the notes *you* made when you brainstormed under similar headings and subheadings.

Plan

Improving amenities

1 Accommodation
More short breaks, discounts at hotels for large parties, build a youth hostel

2 Parking
Build more car parks, introduce 'park and ride' system.

3 Visitor centre
Open a centre with audio-visual show, local historians, artists etc. to tell tourists about the area.

Advertising
Advertise in national press & TV, and in travel agencies abroad

7 Think about your introduction

Look at the exam question again, then read the three introductory paragraphs (a–c) below. Which would make the best introduction to the proposal? Why? What is wrong with the others?

a **Introduction**: Here is my proposal.

b **Introduction**: I would like to put forward the following proposal, which I believe would help to attract more visitors to our area.

c **Introduction:** I think there are lots of ways to attract tourists to this area.

tip

You should start your proposal with an introductory sentence which states the purpose of your proposal *in brief*.

8 Think about your conclusion

Look at the exam question again, then read the two concluding paragraphs, a and b, below. Which would make a better conclusion to the proposal? Why? What is wrong with the other one?

a **Conclusion:** This proposal will involve large initial expenditure. However, the income generated by higher levels of tourism will very quickly offset this. I therefore hope my proposal will be given due consideration.

b **Conclusion:** That is the end of my proposal. I trust you enjoyed reading it.

9 Compare two proposals

Imagine you are an examiner. Read the two proposals, A and B, below. Then use these questions to help you to decide which is better. Compare your opinions with a partner. Say which proposal, A or B:

1 addresses all the aspects asked for in the exam question.
2 is logically organised.
3 is divided into clear sections.
4 has section headings.
5 is easy for the reader to follow.
6 has a brief, clear introduction and conclusion.
7 is formal in register.
8 contains a range of complex structures used correctly.
9 contains a good range of vocabulary.
10 contains clear recommendations for future discussion.

Proposal A

I think there are so many ways how we could attract the tourists to this area. The first thing we can make is to do a special video about our area and all the places that are worth to visit. This will show to people all the interesting things tourists can glimpse in our area, included archaeology, famous castles and monuments etc.

Then if we showed this video on TV and in the cinema, people they will want to come and see the place for themselves. It would be better than to give out brochures because on a video you can show what is the place really like and all there is to do and see here. We must convince other countries to show this video too. Then we can attract tourists from abroad as well.

Why not sending some of our staff to promote tourism abroad? We could send speakers and they could give little chats in schools and factories and other workplaces.

In our locality, we should put organised special walks with different themes. Maybe we do 'history walks' or special walks to look at flowers and the nature. We should also make local hotels to give discounted prices for people who come for a short time. For people with young children, we must make special prices and make them know about amenities for children like our parks and swimming pools.

Now may not be a good time for the tourism because people are afraid to travel because of problems in the world. Also, people may not want to spend money now because they are worried for the economy. But the situation it will surely change in the future.

Proposal B

Proposal to increase the level of tourism in this area

Introduction
I would like to put forward the following proposal, which I believe would help to attract more visitors to our area.

Advertising
This area has a great deal to offer the tourist; however, at present it is our country's best-kept secret. I propose we remedy this situation by running an advertising campaign in the newspapers and on television. We could target overseas visitors by advertising in travel agencies abroad and also by broadcasting on foreign television and radio stations.

Improving amenities

1 Accommodation
The shortage of affordable accommodation is a major drawback for visitors. Although we have three prestigious hotels in the town, they cater for wealthy tourists and there are not enough middle-priced hotels. One solution might be to encourage hotels to offer short breaks at discounted prices as well as discounts for large groups. Another possibility would be to provide tourists with lists of Bed and Breakfast establishments. Finally, I propose we look into the possibility of building a youth hostel just outside the town. This would provide suitable accommodation for young people who cannot afford hotel prices.

2 Parking
Parking is a problem in our town. Ideally, I would like to see a 'park and ride' system introduced. Visitors would then park in a designated place outside town and take one of the specially provided buses into the centre. This system has been successfully adopted in many large towns already.

3 Shops and tourist sites
There should be interpreters and guides at all the major tourist sites and shops should ensure that prices are displayed in euros and dollars.

4 Visitor centre
At the moment, there is nowhere visitors can go to learn about the history of our area and what it has to offer. I propose we build a special visitor centre, where we can have audio-visual shows and displays by local historians and artists.

Conclusion
This proposal will involve substantial initial expenditure. However, the income generated by higher levels of tourism will very quickly offset this. I therefore hope my proposal will be given due consideration.

10 Think about language

The phrases listed below are often used in this type of text. Can you find any of the phrases in the model proposal? If so, underline them.

Making recommendations

My first recommendation would be to ...
I would suggest we ...
I propose we (should) ...
I believe that we should ...
This would mean that ...
This would allow us to ...
We could achieve this by ...
We could ...
We should look into the possibility of ...
One possibility might/would be to ...
Another possibility would be to ...
I would like to see ...
It would be worthwhile to ...
It would be a good idea to ...

tip

When you write a proposal, you have to focus on the future. Make sure you know which grammatical structures you can use to *analyse* a situation, to *recommend* certain steps and to *predict* the results.

11 Exam practice: Write a proposal

You are going to write a proposal. Read the exam question and follow the instructions below.

Part 2

Write your answer in **300–350 words** in an appropriate style.

You work for a large department store. In recent months, sales at the store have fallen. The manager of the store has asked you to think of ways to reverse the situation and to write a proposal. Within your proposal you should include ideas on how to improve the appearance of the store and suggest activities or events that could be staged to encourage more people to come to the store.

Write your **proposal**.

- **Read the question**
  Read the question carefully and underline all the points you must cover.
- **Think about register and style**
  Remember you have a business relationship with your manager. Your proposal should be formal and businesslike and easy for him or her to follow.
- **Think about format**
  Divide your proposal into clear sections with headings. Paragraph longer sections where appropriate.
- **Think about language**
  Use the language you have seen in this unit for making recommendations.

14 Writing a proposal (2)

1 Read the question

Read the exam question below carefully.

Part 1

You **must** answer this question. Write your answer in **300–350 words** in an appropriate style.

You work for an international charity. You and your colleagues have each received a copy of this memo from the directors of the organisation.

Memo: To all members of staff

By now you will all have heard of the generosity of the anonymous benefactor who has donated £200,000 to our charity. The directors are now considering whether to target this sum on one large project or on several smaller ones. They are also deliberating whether some of the funds should be kept in reserve to be used in future emergencies. We would like to hear any suggestions you may have on this matter and invite all staff to send in a written proposal to this end. Within your proposal you should include your views on exactly how the funds should be allocated and which projects should benefit, and your justification for the expenditure.

Write your **proposal**.

exam information

In the Writing Paper you may be asked to write a proposal analysing a situation and making recommendations for the future.

2 Think about your reader

Work with a partner. Look at the exam question again and answer the following questions.

1 Who has asked you to write the proposal?

2 For what purpose are you writing this proposal? To make recommendations? To give your opinion? To explain your actions? To hypothesise about the results of the action you recommend? For some other reason?

3 Should your style and tone be
 a formal?
 b informal?

3 Identify the key points in the question

Work with a partner. Look at the instructions (rubric) and the memo again and answer the following questions.

1 According to the exam question, who do you work for?
2 What has this organisation received?
3 Who will decide what to do with the donation?
4 Which two choices must they make?
- .... or ....
- .... or ....

5 Which three major points must you cover in your proposal?
- ....
- ....
- ....

4 Think about vocabulary

a Name one country or continent that has recently suffered from the following:

- famine
- drought
- floods
- a major epidemic

b What sort of natural disasters often lead to emergency appeals from international charities? Add items to the list.

Hurricanes, floods, ...

c Complete the following sentences with words from the box.

appeal	**desperate**	**distressing**	**donation**
malnourished	**raise**	**urgent**	**victims**

1 The company made a generous .... to Oxfam.
2 Our organisation is trying to .... money to fight the famine in Africa.
3 The Red Cross is making an emergency .... for money to help those people affected by the earthquake.
4 You can see that the children are .... because they are thin and pot-bellied.
5 The pictures of starving children were .... to look at.
6 We need to take .... action if we are to avert a disaster.
7 The situation in the flood zone is now .... and many more people may die unless help comes soon.
8 The refugees who are pouring over the border are the innocent .... of this terrible civil war.

14 Writing a proposal (2)

Collocations

d Match the adjectives (1–6) that collocate with the nouns (a–f). There may be more than one answer.

1 urgent	**a** crisis
2 humanitarian	**b** cause
3 starving	**c** plight
4 worthwhile	**d** zone
5 disaster	**e** action
6 desperate	**f** people

e Complete the following sentences with phrases from **d**.

1 We need to take .... if we want to rescue people from the floods.
2 The victims of the disaster are in a(n) ....
3 We are on the verge of a(n) .... of enormous proportions.
4 Most people are willing to give money to a(n) ....
5 Thousands of .... are making their way to the food camps.
6 The area where the earthquake struck has been declared a(n) .... and only emergency services are being allowed there.

5 Brainstorm the topic

Work with a partner and answer the questions. Note down the best ideas.

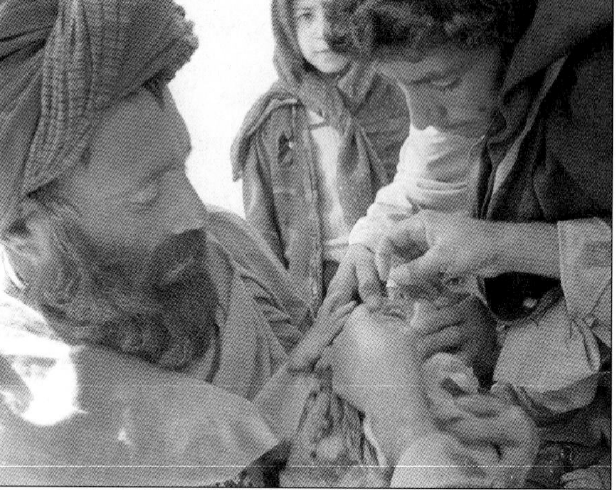

1 Which famous charitable organisations can you name? (e.g. The Red Cross) What do they do?
2 Name three countries/parts of the world which you think are most in need of aid at the moment.
3 Do you remember the last big emergency appeal made by an international charity or charities? Which country/part of the world was affected? What caused the disaster?
4 Imagine you are the head of an international charity. You have been given an unexpected donation of £200,000. How would you spend the money? Would you spend it all on one project or spread it among many projects? Would you keep any money back for future emergencies? If so, why and how much?

Factfile

Greenpeace is an environmental trust that works to further public understanding of world ecology and the natural environment.

Medicins Sans Frontières is an independent medical aid agency committed to providing emergency medical assistance to populations in danger, regardless of race, religion, sex or politics, and to raise awareness of the plight of the people they help. Volunteers travel to every corner of the globe to assist those who have fallen victim to natural or man-made disasters.

Oxfam is a development, relief and campaigning organisation dedicated to finding lasting solutions to poverty and suffering around the world.

The Red Cross and Red Crescent Movement is the world's largest independent humanitarian organisation. It provides protection and assistance for civilians, prisoners of war and the wounded during international wars and internal disturbances. It also provides relief for victims of natural disasters and for refugees and displaced people.

The World Wildlife Fund is the world's largest global conservation organisation. It addresses a range of issues, including survival of wildlife species and their habitats, climate change and environmental education. As well as funding and managing conservation projects throughout the world, the WWF lobbies governments, conducts research, and works with business and industry to address global threats to the planet by seeking long-term solutions for the benefit of people and nature.

6 Make a plan

a Look at the following notes which one student has made. Tick (✓) the points you think she should include in the proposal. Put a cross (✗) against any points that are irrelevant or unimportant.

Notes

1 Should we keep part of this donation in reserve? No! Not necessary!
2 Should we help many projects rather than just one? Yes! It's fairer!
3 What I think is wrong with other well known charitable organisations.
4 Current projects that we should help with these funds:
(1) Aids project
(2) Emergency camps
(3) Drug centres
5 How to raise more money for charities

b Look at the headings the student wrote for her proposal. What is the advantage of writing down clear headings before you start to write a proposal? How will these headings help the reader?

Keeping funds in reserve

One project or many?

Projects:

1 Aids project

2 Emergency camps

3 Drug rehabilitation centre

exam tip

If you start by writing clear section headings, you will find it much easier to write the rest of your proposal.

7 Read a model proposal

Read the model proposal below and answer the following questions.

1. Has the writer divided the proposal into clear sections with clear headings?
2. Has she answered the exam question in full?
3. Has she written anything that is irrelevant?
4. Has she used very basic structures or a range of complex structures? Has she used them correctly?
5. Has she used very basic vocabulary or is there a good range?
6. Is the style and tone appropriate?
7. Will the reader be able to follow her proposal without undue difficulty?
8. Do you think the text has been carefully edited?

Proposal

As requested by the directors, I am submitting the following proposal on how to allocate the money donated to our organisation recently.

Keeping funds in reserve
Reserve funds are extremely important as they enable us to act quickly in the event of a sudden emergency, such as an earthquake or floods. However, given that such a fund already exists, and that we can expect to raise more money in emergency appeals as and when the occasion arises, I suggest that we put this unexpected gift to immediate use.

One project or many?
I believe it would be impossible as well as undesirable to favour one single project or, indeed, one country, above others. For that reason, I would recommend sharing the sum equally among a number of important projects, which I have listed below.

<u>1. Aids project in Africa</u>
Africa must continue to be one of our top priorities. Millions of people are threatened by Aids, and the disease has already killed whole families and left a generation of orphans. The extra funds would allow us to buy medicines, to train more nurses and health workers, and to educate people about the causes of the disease and how to prevent it.

<u>2. Emergency camps</u>
War and drought have forced people in countries like Ethiopia and Afghanistan into refugee camps. With the funds available, we could improve conditions in these camps generally, by providing food, clean water and medical help.

<u>3. Drug rehabilitation centres</u>
Drugs are ruining the lives of young people both in our own country and abroad, so I feel strongly that we should allocate some of the funds to train volunteers. These volunteers would work drug users to help them to conquer their addiction. It would also be possible to set up more centres and run more drug rehabilitation programmes.

8 Think about your conclusion

Which paragraph, a or b, would make a good conclusion? Why? What is wrong with the other one?

a

Conclusion
This is my proposal. I hope it helps you to make up your mind.

b

Conclusion
Having considered the various options, I believe that my proposal is the fairest way of allocating the funds we have been given, and I trust that you will give it due consideration.

tip

Always round off a proposal with finishing remarks, justifying the recommendations you have made and entrusting your conclusions to the reader.

9 Think about language

a Work with a partner and answer the following questions.

1. In a proposal, you will probably make hypothetical statements; in other words, you imagine what the situation *would be* or what *could happen* if your recommendations were followed. Find examples of hypothetical statements in the model text.
2. Underline the phrases the writer uses to give a personal opinion. Can you suggest alternatives?
3. Does the writer always justify her opinions? Find examples in the model text.

b Find words in the model proposal (including the conclusion) that mean the same as the words in italics.

1. In my opinion, it is extremely important to *give out* the money fairly.
2. My colleague believes that we should always have some *money that we put aside for emergencies*.
3. *If there is* a natural disaster of such proportions, many people will die.
4. We will decide what to do *when we are faced with a real-life situation.*
5. It wouldn't be a good idea *to treat* one project *as more important than* another.
6. In relief work of this kind, saving human lives is *one of our most important concerns*.
7. Tragically, many people never *overcome their dependence on a drug*.
8. We hope that you will listen to our point of view and *think about it carefully*.

10 Think about grammar

a Look at the sentences below. Note that we cannot use the *-ing* form of the verb after *propose, suggest* and *recommend* if there is a change of subject.

- We propose/suggest/recommend organising a fund-raising concert. (✓)
- We propose/suggest/recommend that we (should) organise a fund-raising concert. (✓)
- We propose/suggest/recommend all the money from the fund-raising concert going to Afghanistan. (✗)
- We propose/suggest/recommend that all the money from the fund-raising concert goes to Afghanistan. (✓)
- We propose/suggest/recommend that all the money from the fund-raising concert (should) go to Afghanistan. (✓)

b Underline the correct option.

1. I do not recommend *allocating / to allocate* the money to a single important project.
2. They suggested *us to approach / that we approach* large companies and ask them to make a donation.
3. How much money do you expect *to raise / raising* in an emergency?
4. The threat of famine continues *be / to be* one of the continent's biggest problems.
5. We should consider *funding / to fund* more educational programmes to raise awareness of the problem.
6. I propose *us to use / that we use* the money to help refugees.
7. It would be a good idea *to invest / investing* some of the money.
8. It would not be fair *using / to use* all the money on one project.

c Complete the sentences below using the words in brackets. (Sometimes there is more than one possible answer.)

1. I suggest .... (one of our representatives/go out) to Africa immediately.
2. I propose .... (well-known public figures/make) a special appeal on television.
3. We recommend .... (people/make) regular contributions to their favourite charity.
4. Local aid workers have suggested .... (the public/help) by donating money and blankets.
5. We would like to propose .... (spend) a portion of this month's budget advertising our charity.

11 Exam practice: Write a proposal

You are going to write an proposal. Read the exam question and follow the instructions below.

Part 1

You **must** answer this question. Write your answer in **300–350 words** in an appropriate style.

After a recent inspection of your school, the head teacher received a report, an extract from which you can see below. The school has now been allocated substantial extra funds to spend. The head of the school has asked you and other members of the student committee to submit a written proposal, giving your views on how the money should be spent in the light of the comments made in the report.

> It is clear that while the staff are dedicated and hard-working, the school premises, facilities and equipment leave a lot to be desired. The classrooms and corridors look dilapidated, the staff room is small and crowded, and the laboratories and computer rooms appear to be under-equipped and out of date. There do not appear to be any after-school clubs or societies for students, or any extracurricular activities that would awaken students' interest in the world outside the classroom.

Write your **proposal**.

- **Identify the key points in the question**
  1. What is your role in the school?
  2. Who wrote the extract?
  3. What did they say about: (a) the classrooms and corridors? (b) the laboratories and computer rooms? (c) other facilities in the school?
  4. What other aspect of the school did they criticise?
  5. What must you cover in your proposal?

- **Brainstorm the topic**
  Note down ways in which you would use the new funds to rectify the problems.
- **Make a plan**
  Think of four main headings you could use in your proposal. Then group the notes you made when you brainstormed under each of your headings.
- **Think about your introduction and conclusion**
  Make sure you write an appropriate introduction. In your conclusion, summarise your arguments briefly and commend your proposal to your reader.
- **Think about format**
  Divide your proposal into clear sections with headings. Use subheadings if necessary to make the proposal clearer.
- **Think about language**
  Use the correct verb forms to make recommendations and hypothetical statements.

15 Writing a proposal (3)

1 Read the question

Read the exam question below carefully.

Part 1

You **must** answer this question. Write your answer in **300–350 words** in an appropriate style.

You work for a large company. The extract below comes from a memo which was circulated by one of the managers. The Human Resources Director has now asked staff representatives to submit a written proposal, suggesting ways to deal with the problems outlined in the extract and justifying any expenditure involved.

> In common with most of the population, our staff tend to lead extremely unhealthy lifestyles. Far too many exist on a diet of burgers, chips and pizzas or similar fast foods. Few people exercise as they should, with the majority spending their free time in sedentary activities, such as watching television or playing computer games. Obesity is a widespread problem and there is an increased incidence of heart disease. We need to take urgent steps as a company to encourage our workforce to become fitter and healthier.

Write your **proposal**.

exam information

In the Writing Paper you may be asked to write a proposal analysing a situation and making recommendations for the future.

2 Think about your reader

Work with a partner. Look at the instructions (rubric) in the exam question again and answer the following questions.

1 Who do you work for? What special role do you have among the staff?

2 Where does the extract come from? Who wrote it?

3 Who has asked you to write this proposal?
  a a colleague
  b your employer
  c a person who has a high position

4 Should your language be
  a formal?
  b informal?

5 For what purpose are you writing the proposal? To recommend something? To explain the reason for a state of affairs? To oppose something? For some other reason?

3 Identify the key points in the question

a Work with a partner. Look at the instructions (rubric) in the exam question again. Which two major areas have you been asked to cover in your proposal?

b Now look at the extract in the exam question again and answer the following questions.

1 According to the writer of the memo, what is wrong with the staff? What does he/she imply about (a) the food they eat and (b) the amount of exercise they get?
2 What is the result of this unhealthy lifestyle?
3 What does the writer think the company should do?

4 Think about format

Now study the list below. Tick (✓) the features that you could expect to find in most formal proposals.

- addresses
- text divided into sections
- headings
- sub-headings
- an impersonal tone
- direct speech
- recommendations for future actions
- idiomatic language
- complex sentences
- slang
- hypothetical statements
- sophisticated vocabulary used with precision
- passive forms
- a conversational style

5 Think about vocabulary

Collocations

a Which verb collocates with all the words and phrases below?

exercise
time
advantage of something
a shower
advice
steps
a break

b How many different verbs can you think of to complete the sentences below?

1 We could .... a health campaign.
2 We could .... special exercise classes.
3 We should .... people to eat a healthier diet.
4 We should .... a gymnasium on the premises.
5 The benefits would .... the expenditure.

c Complete the following sentences with words from the box.

benefits campaign common facilities practical substantial

1 We could run a health ....
2 We need to take .... steps to help our staff get fitter.
3 It is .... practice for our staff to work over lunchtime.
4 There are clear health .... to taking regular exercise.
5 We should provide exercise ....
6 A .... number of our people on our staff have never used a gym.

6 Brainstorm the topic

Work with a partner and answer the questions. Note down the best ideas.

1 Do you think that people tend to lead an unhealthy lifestyle these days? In what way?
2 Why do you think people eat fast food? Is fast food healthy? Why/Why not?
3 How do you think people might be persuaded to adopt a healthier diet?
4 Why do you think people prefer sedentary activities to exercising? How might this affect their health?
5 How could people be persuaded to take more exercise?
6 Imagine you work for a company. What suggestions would you make to get the staff fitter and healthier?

7 Make a plan

Organise the ideas you brainstormed under the following headings. You can add subheadings.

Plan

Introduction
(reason for writing the proposal and topic)

Diet

Exercise

Expenditure

Conclusion
(brief summary/justification and commend proposal to the director)

8 Compare two proposals

Imagine you are an examiner. Read the two proposals, A and B, below and decide which is better. Justify your choice by picking out weaknesses in the other proposal.

Proposal A

Introduction

As requested, I am submitting the following proposal on how to encourage our workforce to become fitter and healthier.

Diet

1. Health education

A number of our staff appear to be unaware of the consequences of eating fried fatty food. I recommend that we run our own health campaign, with posters and leaflets, to encourage people to eat a healthier diet.

2. Practical steps

In the meantime, we should take some practical steps. Many members of staff are in the habit of working through their lunchtime. It is common practice for them to order a burger or pizza, which they eat at their desks. I propose that we encourage staff to take a proper break and to go to the staff restaurant where healthier foods such as salads would be included on the menu.

Exercise

1. The current situation

When questioned, most workers said they were aware of the health benefits of exercising and the dangers of obesity. However, it is a fact that some of our staff commute considerable distances in order to get to work, which means that they have limited leisure time in the evenings. If we were to offer exercise facilities at work, it appears that a substantial number of people would be ready to take advantage of these.

2. Practical steps

I suggest we set up a staff gymnasium with showers and a coffee bar, which people could use either before or after work or during the lunch period. Staff would then have the opportunity to exercise on the premises without inconvenience or expense. We should also run after-work classes in aerobics and step dancing and set up a football club to encourage those who would not normally use a gym.

Expenditure

I believe that the long-term benefits to our company would very quickly offset the expenditure involved. Fewer days would be lost to sickness and the work capacity and general morale of the staff would be much higher.

Conclusion

I believe that my proposal is the best way to create a healthier and fitter workforce and I trust you will give it your full consideration.

Proposal B

Dear Sir or Madam,

Here is my proposal. I believe it will help us to make our staff fitter and healthier.

Diet

A major problem is that some of our staff do not have a clue about the importance of diet. We must run our own health scheme. If people realise that fatty foods are bad for them, they will stop eating them. I reckon we should run a campaign. We can make posters and leaflets and show people how their health will improve if they eat more vegetables and fruit. Why not get staff to take a proper break instead of having working lunches all the time? That way, they wouldn't eat so much fast food.

Exercise

Most of our staff know they should exercise more. They know all about the dangers of obesity and heart problems. The problem is they have to commute long distances to work, so they don't have time to go to a gym or to exercise classes when they get home.

What about setting up a gym here at work? Then they could exercise here before and after work and it will save them going out again when they get home.

It will cost the company money in the beginning because we will have to build the gym and get equipment, but we will get the money back in the end because everyone will be fitter.

Conclusion

I hope you will find my proposal helpful.

9 Think about language

a Most proposals will usually analyse a current situation, recommend a course of action and make hypothetical statements about the future. Underline the words or phrases that the writer of **Proposal A** uses to make (a) recommendations and (b) hypothetical statements.

b Find words in **Proposal A** that mean the same as the words in italics.

1. My colleagues and I are *putting in* our proposal tomorrow.
2. The *people who work in a company* deserve to be treated fairly and with consideration. (2 possible answers)
3. The company is going to build a new gym for its employees. *Between now and the time when it is ready*, they will still be able to use the old one.
4. We *tend to work* with music playing in the background.
5. *It is usual* for them to have coffee after a meal.
6. A number of us live on the outskirts of the city, so we *travel a long way to work*.
7. The advantages of the scheme will definitely *compensate for* the drawbacks.

10 Exam practice: Write a proposal

You are going to write an proposal. Read the exam question and follow the instructions below.

Part 1

You **must** answer this question. Write your answer in **300–350 words** in an appropriate style.

You work part time in your local library. The extract below comes from a report which inspectors wrote after a recent visit there. The head librarian has asked each member of staff to submit a written proposal based on the extract, outlining ideas for improving the library and justifying any expenditure involved.

> Although the staff are generally well qualified, the library itself is dingy and uninspiring. There is a good range of books but there is little in the way of information to let readers know about new publications or to interest them in particular subjects. A modern library should offer a range of facilities, not least of which should be access to information technology. We were disappointed to discover that there is only one computer available to users of the library, and that it was out of order. There were no educational programmes to help the public to familiarise themselves with the new technology, and no staff trained to assist in case of queries in this area.

Write your **proposal**.

- **Read the question**
  1 Where do you work?
  2 Who has asked you to write a proposal?
  3 Which main areas should you cover in your proposal?
  4 What criticism did the report make about
     a the premises?
     b the information that is available about books?
     c the facilities as a whole?
     d access to technology?
     e specialised staff?
- **Think about register and style**
  Remember that you have a business relationship with your employer. Your proposal should be formal and businesslike and easy for him or her to follow.
- **Think about format**
  Remember that your proposal must be logically organised and easy for the reader to follow. Divide your proposal into clear sections with headings, and, if necessary, subheadings.
- **Think about your introduction and conclusion**
  Remember that a proposal has a clear introduction and conclusion. Look at Proposal A on page 101 to remind yourself of this.
- **Think about language**
  Your proposal must contain clear recommendations for future discussion. Use appropriate verb forms to make hypothetical statements about the future.

16 Writing a report (1)

1 Read the question

Read the exam question below carefully.

Part 2

Write your answer in **300–350 words** in an appropriate style.

You work for a busy hotel. Over recent weeks, there have been complaints about various aspects of the hotel. The manager has now asked you to write a report, reviewing the complaints and suggesting how the situation can be improved.

Write your **report**.

exam information

Reports only occur in Part 2 of the Writing Paper.

2 Think about your reader

Work with a partner. Look at the exam question again and answer the following questions.

1 Who is going to read your report?
- **a** a colleague
- **b** a guest
- **c** your employer

2 Should your report be
- **a** formal?
- **b** informal?

3 For what purpose are you writing? To apologise? To describe something? To make excuses? To make suggestions?

4 Which two areas must you cover in your report?

3 Think about format

Study the templates A and B below. Which is suitable for your report?

Template A

57 Cypress Ave
Twickenham
London EC3 8TB

3/10/2002

Dear Sir or Madam,

………………………………………………………………………………

………………………………………….

Yours faithfully,

Template B

To:

From:

Subject:

Introduction

....

Rooms

1 ....

2 ....

Staff

....

Restaurant

....

Conclusion

....

4 Brainstorm the topic

a Work with a partner and answer the questions.

1 Describe the problems in the hotel in the picture.

2 Describe the best and worst hotels you have ever stayed in. If you have never stayed in a hotel, say what you imagine could go wrong.

b Make notes about your complaints of the worst hotel you have stayed in (real or imaginary) in the following sections.

Staff: *Rude, unhelpful. Didn't offer to help us with luggage. Didn't have time to listen to our complaints.*

Entertainment: *Too noisy. We couldn't sleep at night because of the disco.*

Facilities: ....

Food: ....

Price: ....

c Now imagine you are the manager of the hotel and have just received the complaints you made in **b**. What steps do you think you could take to solve the hotel's problems? What suggestions might you make to your boss, the owner of the hotel? Make some notes.
e.g. *We should improve the soundproofing in the disco.*

16 Writing a report (1)

5 Think about vocabulary

a Match the words (1–10) with their opposites (a–j).

1 airy	**a** cramped
2 spotless	**b** rude
3 efficient	**c** exorbitant
4 good-humoured	**d** out of order
5 polite	**e** inedible
6 spacious	**f** noisy
7 reasonable	**g** stuffy
8 delicious	**h** disorganised
9 quiet	**i** bad-tempered
10 in working order	**j** filthy

b Complete the following sentences with words from **a**.

1. The guests complained that the disco was too ....
2. The windows wouldn't open, so the room was hot and ....
3. The bathroom was .... and looked as if it hadn't been cleaned.
4. The lift was ...., so the guests had to use the stairs.
5. One guest complained that his room was so .... that he could hardly turn round in it.
6. Most of the staff were polite but one or two were extremely ....
7. Guests complained that prices in the restaurant were ....
8. The chef put too much salt in the vegetables, which meant they were almost ....

c Match the verbs (1–6) with their synonyms (a–f).

1 dismiss	**a** ignore
2 disregard	**b** fire
3 look into	**c** repair
4 put in	**d** install
5 recommend	**e** investigate
6 fix	**f** propose

d Complete the following sentences with the correct form of a verb from **c**. There are two possible answers for each sentence.

1. The lift broke down, and the mechanic wasn't able to .... / .... it.
2. We may have to .... / .... some of the staff unless their attitude improves.
3. We should consider .... / .... a new heating system.
4. We have now .... / .... all the guests' complaints and decided on the measures we should take.
5. I .... / .... that we redecorate the hotel lounge and reception area as soon as possible.
6. A number of guests have complained about the waiter, and we cannot .... / .... what they have said.

6 Think about style

a Look at some of the characteristics of **Formal** and **Informal language** in the boxes below.

Formal language
- neutral tone
- tentative language
- impersonal verbs
- complex sentences
- sophisticated vocabulary used precisely
- passive forms
- diplomatic phrasing
- sentences beginning with participle clauses

Informal language
- direct tone
- personalised verbs
- colloquial expressions
- phrasal verbs
- abbreviations
- very short sentences
- contractions
- extreme language

b Tick (✓) the more formal sentence in each pair of options below.

1 **a** I've had a look into what residents complained about.
b I have now investigated the complaints which were made by residents.

2 **a** I'm going to do the things I've listed here.
b I plan to implement the measures listed.

3 **a** When we had a look at the radiators, we found that two weren't working.
b On checking the radiators, we found that two were out of order.

4 **a** The customer was given a room at the back of the hotel, where the noise level is low.
b We put the customer at the back of the hotel, where it's quieter.

5 **a** Why don't we put large groups in a separate annexe?
b One solution could be to allocate rooms for large groups in a separate annexe.

6 **a** I recommend that we look into the possibility of fitting a new lift.
b We ought to fit a new lift.

7 **a** It should be done as a matter of urgency.
b We should do it quickly.

8 **a** The staff proved to be unable to cope with the demands of the job.
b The staff were useless.

C Rewrite the sentences below in a more formal style. Use the correct form of the verbs in the box to replace the informal verbs and expressions. Make any necessary changes.

allocate	cope	disregard	experience difficulty	propose	rectify

Informal/spoken style	Formal written style
e.g. We've *got rid of* the faulty lamps. →	*The lamps which were faulty have been replaced.*
1 Some guests have been *taking no notice* of the no smoking signs.	....
2 We *gave* the guests special rooms on the ground floor.	....
3 I *vote* we ban smoking in the restaurant.	....
4 We've *fixed* most of the problems.	....
5 We've *had trouble* getting staff.	....
6 The staff *aren't up to* the job.	....

7 Make a plan

The exam question requires you to imagine that guests have complained about several aspects of your hotel. Write down four or five headings like those below. Then note down the complaints that have been made and what you suggest should be done.

<u>**Plan**</u>

Rooms

1 Complaint: *Guests are cold.*
Suggested solution: *Overhaul heating system.*

2 Complaint: ....
Suggested solution: ....

Noise

Complaint: ....
Suggested solution: ....

Food

Complaint: ....
Suggested solution: ....

Staff and service

Complaint: ....
Suggested solution: ....

8 Read a model report

Read the report below. Use the checklist to help you to decide if is well written.

A well-written report:

- has a clear introduction and conclusion.
- is clearly organised.
- is divided into sections.
- has clear headings.
- often includes numbered subheadings.
- is clear and easy to follow.
- is impersonal in tone.
- is formal in style.

REPORT

To:	Mr K. Brown	**Date:**	31 August, 200-
From:	Patricia Smith		
Subject:	Recent complaints regarding Harbour Lights Hotel		

Introduction

The purpose of this report is to review the recent complaints made about the hotel and to suggest the steps we should take to improve the situation.

Rooms

A number of guests have complained that their rooms are cold. Checks have revealed that radiators in some rooms are faulty and in two *they* are completely out of order.

Suggested action:

I suggest we look into the cost of installing a brand new heating system in the near future. In the interim, I propose that we install new radiators in the rooms in question.

Noise

There have been several complaints about the noise from the disco. *This* is sound-proofed, of course but *it* is open to non-residents, and *they* tend to gather outside in the street after *it* closes, which may explain *the problem*.

Suggested action:

I recommend that we restrict entrance to the disco to hotel residents and their guests. I also suggest that we should close *it* an hour earlier than at present, at midnight.

The Restaurant

1. Staff

Complaints *here* have been about the long delays in getting served at peak times. There have been difficulties recently because of staff shortages. However, we are now back to our full complement of staff and I do not envisage any further problems in *this area*.

2. Smoking

This is a major problem. While we have allocated a no smoking zone, most guests disregard signs and persist in smoking in *this area.*

Suggested action:

I propose we make the whole restaurant a no smoking area and implement the ban more forcefully. We could then designate one corner of the bar as a smoking area.

Conclusion

Most of the problems highlighted by the complaints will be quite straightforward to solve. We have already rectified problems in some areas and await your approval to act on the outstanding issues.

16 Writing a report (1)

9 Link your text

a Look back at the model report on page 109. The words in *italics* help to link the text together. Highlight the words or information they refer back to in the text.

b Choose the most suitable word or phrase to link the following sentences.

1 [Despite / However / While] it is a fact that the hotel is expensive, it is [nevertheless / beside / although] the most comfortable and luxurious place you could stay in.

2 The lifts are very old. They are, [so / consequently / for all that], somewhat unreliable.

3 [Although / Nonetheless / Despite] the complaints sound serious, I believe they can be easily dealt with.

4 [Overall / All over / In total], I am of the opinion that this hotel is of the highest standard.

5 Staff have been under tremendous pressure. [In spite of / Although / Nevertheless], they have coped extremely well.

6 We cannot provide the same services as the major hotels; we are tiny, [conversely / furthermore / whereas] they are huge.

10 Think about vocabulary

Find words and phrases in the model text which mean the same as the words below.

1 for the time being ....
2 to limit ....
3 the busiest times ....
4 all the staff we should have ....
5 to imagine ....
6 to continue ....
7 to put into effect ....
8 to set aside ....
9 put right ....
10 things that have not yet been dealt with ....

11 Exam practice: Write a report

You are going to write a report. Read the exam question and follow the instructions below.

Part 2

Write your answer in **300–350 words** in an appropriate style.

You work at a leisure centre. Recently, members have complained about various aspects of the centre including the sports facilities and the cafeteria. There have also been complaints about parking arrangements outside the centre. The manager has asked you to write a report, reviewing the complaints and recommending steps to be taken to remedy the situation.

Write your **report**.

- **Make a plan**
  Your report must be well organised and easy to follow. Making a detailed plan before you start writing will help you with this.
- **Think about format**
  Remember that your report must be divided into sections with clear headings. Use numbered subheadings where appropriate. Make sure you include separate sections for your introduction and conclusion.
- **Think about style**
  Remember that reports are usually impersonal documents which are formal or neutral in style. Use impersonal forms and passive forms where appropriate.

17 Writing a report (2)

1 Read the question

Read the exam question below carefully.

Part 2

Write your answer in **300–350 words** in an appropriate style.

You are employed as a researcher by your local tourist office. Your manager has asked you to write a report on two contrasting restaurants, which you would recommend to visitors, both from your own country and abroad. Within your report you should include comments on the size and location of the restaurants as well as the atmosphere, service and type of dishes served.

Write your **report**.

exam information

In the exam, you may be asked to write a report comparing or contrasting two places.

2 Think about your reader

Work with a partner. Look at the exam question again and answer the following questions.

1 Who has asked you to write this report?
   a a tourist
   b a colleague
   c your superior

2 For what purpose are you writing the report? To advertise the restaurants? To compare and contrast them? To give information about them?

3 Why does the reader want the information you supply in the report?

4 Should your report be
   a informal?
   b formal?

3 Identify the key points in the question

Work with a partner. Look at the exam question again and answer the following questions.

1 How many restaurants are you asked to write about?

2 Are you asked to comment on similar restaurants or contrasting ones?

3 Does the manager want you to write about restaurants that are good or ones that are not very good?

4 Are you expected to recommend one or both of the restaurants?

5 Which aspects of the restaurants must you include in your report? Underline them in the exam question.

exam tip

Note that in this question, you are asked to recommend two good restaurants, not to recommend one above the other. Read the exam question very carefully before you start to write and make sure you know exactly what you are being asked to do.

4 Think about vocabulary

a The words and phrases below can all be used to describe food. Tick (✓) those which have a positive or neutral meaning and put a cross (✗) next to those that have a negative meaning. (Some can be both positive and negative, depending on the context.)

crisp delicious disappointing dried-up exotic fatty fresh greasy healthy imaginative limp melt-in-the-mouth mouth-watering overcooked plain raw spicy stale stunning succulent superb tasteless tender tough

b Write down pairs of words with an opposite meaning.
e.g. *crisp/limp*

c Write the words and phrases below in the correct category.

attentive central pricey convenient reasonably-priced cosy courteous cramped efficient friendly off the beaten track offhand over-priced roomy sophisticated spacious

Size: ....

Price: ....

Service/Staff: ....

Location: ....

Atmosphere: ....

d Complete the following sentences with an appropriate word or phrase from **a** or **c**. (Sometimes more than one answer is possible.)

1 Although the meal was rather ...., (thank goodness I had been to the bank before I went!), the quality of the food was superb.

2 It is a highly .... restaurant, full of men in dinner jackets and ladies in designer dresses.

3 The steak in the first restaurant was rather tough. The steak in the second restaurant, however, was so .... that it melted in the mouth!

4 While the staff in the first restaurant I visited were very offhand, I found the waiters in the second restaurant extremely ....

5 The desserts were ....; I could hardly wait to bite into my almond and apricot meringue.

6 Although the restaurant was rather .... (it took us half an hour of map-reading to find it!), it was well worth the search.

7 The food at the new Thai restaurant is very hot and ...., so if you like plain food, don't go there.

8 One restaurant has a log fire which makes the whole place feel warm and ....

17 Writing a report (2)

5 Brainstorm the topic

1 The Lemon Tree

2 The Green Lodge

a Describe each of the restaurants in the pictures above. Try to include some of the words and phrases from **4 Think about vocabulary**.

b Imagine what it would be like to eat at the restaurants above. Make notes about each restaurant in the following tables.

1 The Lemon Tree

Size	Location	Type of dishes	Prices	Staff and service	Atmosphere

2 The Green Lodge

Size	Location	Type of dishes	Prices	Staff and service	Atmosphere

exam tip

It is important that you write a balanced report. In this case, you need to give equal attention to both restaurants.

6 Think about language

Look back at the pictures of the two restaurants on p.114. Write sentences comparing and contrasting them, using the language in the box.

e.g. *Unlike The Green Lodge, The Lemon Tree is light and spacious.*

Comparing and contrasting

One of the main differences between (X) and (Y) is that ...

(X) is totally/entirely/completely different from (Y), in that ...

Unlike (X), (Y) is ...

While (X) is ..., (Y) is ...

Whereas (X) is ..., (Y) is ...

Although (X) is ..., (Y) is ...

(X) is not quite as ... as (Y) because ...

(X) is a little/slightly/rather/somewhat/a great deal/considerably (bigger/more elegant) than (Y).

The (price) at (X) is virtually/more or less/approximately/exactly the same as at (Y).

7 Think about style

Underline the words or phrases in the text below that you would not expect to see in a formal report.

Size and location

The Capri is a great big, sophisticated restaurant in one of the most fashionable parts of town. It is really, really popular so it is advisable to book well ahead, especially at the weekend.

Atmosphere

This restaurant is extremely posh. When I popped in at 7.30 last Saturday night, it was already bustling with diners; the women wearing designer dresses, the men dressed up like a dog's dinner.

Price

I got the fright of my life when I finally received the bill. This restaurant is really pricey, but the food is great, so I suppose it is worth the expense.

17 Writing a report (2)

8 Make a plan

a Look back at the exam question on p.112. Decide how you are going to group the aspects you are asked to comment on, how many sections you are going to have in your report, and what headings you are going to include.

b Complete the plan below. (The headings are given as examples and you can change them if you wish.)

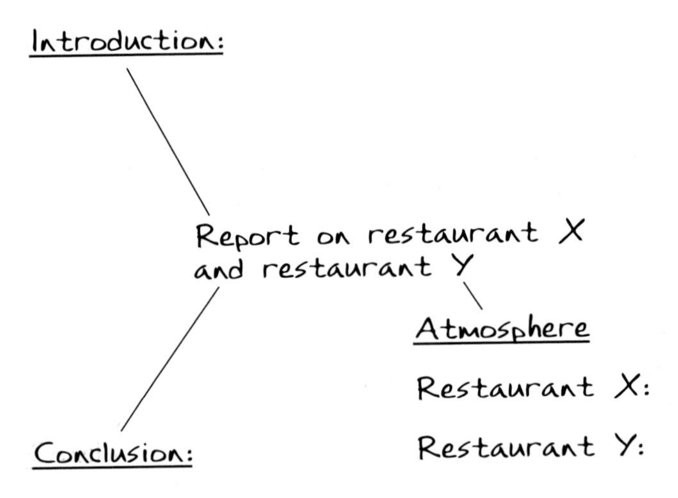

9 Think about your introduction

a A report often begins with the headings opposite. Look back at the exam question on p.112 and complete the introductory section with suitable information.

b Look at the four introductions below. Choose the one which is appropriate for the formal report in the exam question. Say what is wrong with each of the others, e.g. Number (1):

- is too long
- is too short
- contains the wrong information
- is unclear
- is too informal

To:

From: Date:

Subject:

1 *Here's the report you asked me for. Hope it's OK!*

2 This is a report on one of the restaurants we plan to recommend.

3 I have now visited both of the restaurants we plan to recommend in the forthcoming brochure and have prepared the following report for your consideration.

4 I have now visited both of the restaurants we plan to recommend in the forthcoming brochure and I have moreover prepared the following report for your consideration which I very much hope you will find satisfactory and I will naturally be pleased to supply any other information you require whenever convenient and I await your reply and your reactions to this report.

C Write an appropriate introduction for the following topics.

1 The company you work for has decided to offer sports membership of a sports centre as a benefit to its employees. You have been asked by your employer to write a report on two sports centres in the area and to recommend the better one.

2 You work for an agency that arranges short courses for students in foreign countries. The agency has asked you to visit two very different schools and to write a report comparing them and recommending the better one.

10 Think about your conclusion

Look at the four conclusions below. Choose the one which is appropriate for the formal report in the exam question on p.112. Say what is wrong with each of the others.

1 While I can recommend the first restaurant wholeheartedly, I could not do the same for the second. I believe we should investigate another establishment.

2 Both restaurants were great! I recommend both of them.

3 Although the restaurants are quite different, I found them both to be excellent and have no hesitation in recommending them.

4 I found both restaurants, while they are quite different, excellent and would recommend them wholeheartedly because I think that both for food and for atmosphere as well as for many other aspects they could not be bettered.

Useful phrases for reports

This report contains my comments on …

This report deals with …

I have now … and submit the following report for your consideration.

My overall recommendation/opinion/feeling is that …

On the whole, I believe we can …

I have no hesitation in recommending …

11 Edit your text

Read the report below and correct the errors in it, using the following code to help you.

Correction code

SP – spelling	WW – wrong word	X – word not needed
P – punctuation	WF – wrong form	^ – word/punctuation missing
WO – word order	T – tense	

INTERNAL REPORT

To:	Head of Tourism	**Date:**	6 September, 199-
From:	Paul Mason		
Subject:	Restaurants to be recommended in our next brochure		

Introduction

This report contains my comments at [WW] the two restaurants, The Capri and The Green Man, which I believe we should recomend [SP] on [WW] the forthcoming brochure.

Size and location

1 The Capri is a spacious [^] airy restaurant on [WW] the centre of the town. It can sit [WW] a maximum of eighty people, inside and on the terrace at the back [^] which has a tremendous scene [WW] over the town.

X 2 The Green Man is a small and family restaurant tucked away in [WW] the outskirts of town. While it is a little off the beaten track, it is well worth to visit [WF] as it has an atmosphere marvellously relaxed and cosy. [WO] It can sit [WW] a maximum of thirty people, althought [SP] in the summer there is a chance to eat at [WW] the garden if the weather permit. [WF]

Types of dishes

1 The Capri is catering [T] for sophisticated tastes. It provides an imaginative range of dishes including such delicacies as caviar [^] wild salmon and venison together with a good variation [WW] of mouth-watering deserts. [SP]

2 In spite of [WW] The Green Man does not provide the same range of dishes, it does offers [WF] a delicious home-cooked menue, [SP] with succulent steaks and chicken dishes for meat-eaters and a variety of imaginative dishes for vegetarians.

Atmosphere and service

Whereas The Capri offers an atmosphere which is and [WW] elegant and sophisticated, The Green Man is cosy and friendly, with log fires in winter. The standard of service in both is excellent.

Prices

As you might expect, prices in The Capri are much more higher than in The Green Man. While this is, of course, an important difference between the two, both give the good value for money. X

Conclusion

Although the two restaurants are very different, I found them to be both [WO] excellent and have no hesitation from [WW] recommending them to tourists visiting our town.

tip

It is important to begin and end your report in an effective way. This will help your reader to follow the text and be sure about what you are recommending.

12 Exam practice: Write a report

You are going to write a report. Read the exam question and follow the instructions below.

Part 2

Write your answer in **300–350** words in an appropriate style.

You work for a firm that organises language courses for students in your town. Your manager has asked you to write a report, recommending two schools which are very different in character, but which both offer value for money. Write your report, commenting on aspects of the schools including size, location, facilities, and staffing.

Write your **report**.

exam tip

When you write a report, you can invent information, but make sure you cover the aspects mentioned in the exam question.

- **Brainstorm the topic**
  If possible, think about language schools you know. Make notes on the aspects mentioned in the exam question. Add other aspects, if necessary.
- **Make a plan**
  Check through your notes. Decide which are essential. You cannot include too many points in your report, so cross out any ideas that are unimportant or irrelevant.
- **Think about format**
  Remember how to head a report. Divide your report into sections with headings. Write a clear introduction and conclusion.
- **Think about style**
  Use formal language. Include impersonal forms and passive forms where appropriate.

18 Writing a film review

1 Read the question

Read the exam question below carefully.

exam information

Reviews only occur in Part 2 of the Writing Paper. You may be asked to write a review of a film, play, television programme or book.

Part 2

Write your answer in **300–350 words** in an appropriate style.

One of your favourite novels has just been turned into a film. Write a review of the film for a quality media magazine, and comment on how successful the dramatisation has been.

Write your **review**.

exam tip

The exam question may contain two or more aspects. Read the question carefully and give each aspect sufficient emphasis in your review.

2 Think about your reader

Work with a partner. Look at the exam question again and answer the following questions.

1 Most of the readers of your review will be
  a friends.
  b strangers.
  c colleagues.

2 What do you know about your readers?

3 What sort of publication are you writing for?
  a a school magazine
  b a tabloid newspaper
  c a quality magazine

4 What style should you use for your review?
  a informal
  b neutral/quite formal

5 For what purpose are you writing? To compare two things? To give an opinion? To justify your views? To inform? To interest? For some other reason?

3 Identify the key points in the question

You have to do *two* main things in your review. What are they? Underline them in the exam question.

4 Think about vocabulary

a Complete the following sentences with words from the box.

based **cast** **directed** **scene** **set** **shot** **theme** **villain**

1 The film *Captain Corelli's Mandolin* was .... on location in Greece.
2 The well-known American actor, Nicholas Cage, is .... in the leading role.
3 The film *Schindler's List* was .... by Steven Spielberg.
4 Love is the major .... of the film.
5 The film *Enigma* is .... on a novel by Robert Harris.
6 Tom Cruise turns out to be a hero but Alan Rickman is an out and out ....
7 My favourite .... is the one where the two lovers meet again after the war is over.
8 *Jurassic Park* is .... on a tropical island and takes place at some time in the near future.

b Work with a partner and answer the following questions.

1 Can you name a recent **blockbuster**?
2 Can you hum a well-known film **score?**
3 What is the **ending** of *Romeo and Juliet*?
4 Can you describe a video **clip** that is often shown on television?
5 Can you name a film that is full of **suspense**?
6 Can you name three films which are famous for their **special effects**?
7 Can you name one well-known **thriller** and one **disaster movie**?
8 Do you prefer **science fiction films** or **love stories**?

Collocations

c Complete the following sentences with words from the box that collocate with the words in *italics*.

atmosphere **character** **climax** **cuts** **escape** **foreboding** **scene** **spellbinding** **turn** **unfolds**

1 Let me *set the* .... for you.
2 I thought Nicole Kidman *portrayed the* .... of the heroine very well.
3 The director has managed to *capture the* .... of post-war London superbly.
4 The scriptwriter had to *make* .... otherwise the film would have been too long.
5 Halfway through the film, events *take an unexpected* ....
6 Penelope Cruz gives *a(n)* .... *performance* which may win her an Oscar.
7 As *the plot* ...., we discover that the policeman is actually a crook.
8 Events *build to a(n)* .... when soldiers arrive in the town.
9 *An air of* .... pervades the film.
10 The hero has *a narrow* .... when his car is ambushed.

18 Writing a film review

5 Brainstorm the topic

Work with a partner and answer the questions. Note down the best ideas.

1 How many films can you name that are based on novels?

2 List some of the problems you think a film maker faces when he or she dramatises a novel. Think about the following:
- **a** the setting
- **b** the atmosphere
- **c** the characters
- **d** the plot
- **e** the expectations of the audience

3 Think of a film you have seen that is based on a book.
- **a** Where is it set?
- **b** Who are the main characters?
- **c** What is the plot?
- **d** How well did the film capture the atmosphere of the book?
- **e** Were the characters just as you had pictured them from your reading of the book?
- **f** Had any events been changed?
- **g** Were you impressed or disappointed by the dramatisation?

6 Make a plan

Look at the paragraph plan one student made for his review. What does he need to cover in Paragraph 4?

Paragraph 1 / Introduction
Name of the film and book. Where they are set and period in which they are set.

Paragraph 2
The plot

Paragraph 3
The director and cast

Paragraph 4
....

7 Read a model review

a Read the review below. Use the checklist to help you to decide if it is well written.

A well-written review:

- is informative.
- is interesting.
- contains some element of judgement.
- is written in an appropriate register.
- contains well-developed paragraphs.
- has a well-developed introduction and conclusion.
- may contain narrative and/or descriptive language.
- may contain the language of evaluation.
- may contain a wide range of vocabulary relating to the cinema, theatre, television or books.

tip

We normally use present tenses to summarise the story of a book or film.

This week's film: *Captain Corelli's Mandolin*

Captain Corelli's Mandolin is the latest blockbuster to hit our cinemas. Based on the novel by Louis de Bernieres, it is set in the idyllic Greek island of Cephalonia at the time of the Second World War.

It is, at heart, a love story. The Italian army are occupying Cephalonia, but they are not at ease with their position as conquerors. Although they are clearly enjoying the local delights (wine, women and song), they apologise frequently to their hosts for being there at all. One officer, Captain Corelli, hates war. He is humorous, loving and gentle and he loves life, opera, and most of all, his beloved mandolin. He is billeted at the house of the genial local doctor, who has a beautiful daughter called Pelagia. Inevitably, the two young people are attracted to each other, even though Pelagia is already engaged to a handsome young partisan called Mandras. But then events take an unexpected turn.

Directed by John Madden, the film captures all the beauty of the Greek island, with its clear blue skies and sun-drenched beaches. It has a quality cast, with Nicholas Cage as the hero and the stunningly beautiful Penelope Cruz as Pelagia. John Hurt gives a spellbinding performance as Pelagia's father, the doctor. The film score, with a mandolin solo, is both enchanting and evocative.

While film goers will undoubtedly love the film, those who have read the novel may feel disappointed. The book is long and is rich in details and events. Only a few of these are portrayed in the film, and the cuts have been quite drastic. Fans of the novel may also feel cheated by the changes that have been made. Physically at least, Nicholas Cage does not fit the description of Corelli, for example. The problem, as with most dramatisations, is that readers have built a picture of the main characters in their own imagination. Squaring this with what they see on screen may be a bigger challenge than some can overcome.

b Look back at the exam question. Does the model review cover the two areas specified? Does the writer of the review give enough attention to both? Find the sections of the review that relate to those areas.

c Which tenses does the writer use to outline the plot? Underline examples in the model review.

d Which tenses does the writer use to describe the film (Paragraph 3)? Underline examples.

e Is there a topic sentence in each paragraph? Underline examples.

8 Think about vocabulary

Find words and phrases in the model review which mean the same as the words below.

1 happy and peaceful with no problems or dangers ....
2 feeling comfortable and confident ....
3 cheerful and friendly ....
4 extreme ....
5 making something fit ....

9 Think about language

Contrasting

a Join the sentences starting with the word given.

1 Film goers will love the film. Readers of the novel may feel disappointed.
While ....

2 The heroine is already engaged. She falls in love with an Italian soldier.
Despite ....

3 Captain Corelli is a soldier. He hates
Although ....

4 The film covers fewer events. It is just as exciting as the book.
In spite ....

5 The novel highlights the role played by other countries in the war. The film glosses over those details.
Whereas ....

Comparing

b Think of a film based on a novel or a television adaptation that you have seen recently and compare it with the original novel, using the words in the box.

The book is *far more/less spine-chilling* than the film.
The film is *much/a little easier* to follow than the book.

a great deal	challenging
a little	detailed
far	easy to follow
much	enthralling
slightly	exciting
	imaginative
	involved
	romantic
	spine-chilling
	straightforward
	thought-provoking
	vivid

10 Exam practice: Write a film review

You are going to write a film review. Read the exam question and follow the instructions below.

Part 2

Write your answer in **300–350 words** in an appropriate style.

A novel you have read has just been made into a film. Write a review of the film for a quality magazine, and comment on the difficulties a film maker faces when adapting such a novel for the big screen.

Write your **review**.

exam tip

Remember that the exam question will probably ask for more than a simple film review, so read the question carefully and make sure you answer it in full.

- **Read the question**
  Underline all the points you must cover in the exam question and give them sufficient coverage in your answer.
- **Think about style and tone**
  Your review should be interesting and informative. You will probably need to use descriptive and/or narrative language.
- **Make a plan**
  Brainstorm the question and make a paragraph plan before you start to write.
- **Think about paragraphing**
  Your review should be divided into clear, logical paragraphs and have an introduction and conclusion.
- **Think about tenses**
  Use present tenses to write about the plot of a film or book.

19 Writing a book review

1 Read the question

Read the exam question below carefully.

Part 2

Write your answer in **300–350 words** in an appropriate style.

You have been reading to a young relative and have just discovered a book which has impressed you for a variety of reasons. Write a review of the book for a magazine and comment on the features that make it an ideal book for children.

Write your **review**.

exam information

In Part 2 of the Writing Paper, you may be asked to write a book review.

2 Think about your reader

Work with a partner. Look at the exam question again and answer the following questions.

1 What relationship do you have with your readers?
  a They are strangers.
  b They are known to you.
  c They are your relatives.
2 Should the style of your review be
  a neutral/formal?
  b informal?
3 For what purpose are you writing your review? To interest? To inform? To evaluate? To give an opinion? For some other reason?

3 Identify the key points in the question

Work with a partner. Look at the exam question again and answer the following questions.

1 What have you just discovered?
2 Who was it written for?
3 What is your opinion of it?
4 What have you been asked to comment on in your review?
5 Underline the two points that you must cover in your answer.

4 Think about vocabulary

a Complete the following sentences with a word from the box.

cast chapters cliff-hanger hardback illustrated marvellous paperback plot scene title

1 The .... of this book is *Pirates Galore*.
2 The author has written a(n) .... tale of piracy and adventure.
3 The book is .... with brilliant pictures by a well-known artist.
4 The book has a rich .... of characters, such as Jason and his pirate friends.
5 The .... is simple: a boy goes to sea, finds his boat taken over by pirates, and has many adventures before he finally returns to his family.
6 I especially liked the .... in which he tries to teach the pirates to read.
7 The book is full of suspense. There are twenty .... and each one ends with a(n) ....
8 The .... edition of the book is much cheaper than the .... edition.

b Rewrite the sentences below replacing the words in italics with a word from the box.

convincing gripping humorous intriguing inventive

1 The book is *funny* at times but it can also be sad.
....
2 The plot is *exciting and full of suspense.*
....
3 I found the description of life on board a pirate ship *believable.*
....
4 The title of the book is *interesting because it is strange and mysterious.*
....
5 The author is *able to think of new, different and interesting ideas.*
....

c Explain the meaning of the phrases in italics in the sentences below.

1 The book was so good *I couldn't put it down.*
2 There was *an unexpected twist to the story.*
3 The author often *leads you down the wrong path.*
4 I would like to tell you a little about the plot but *I mustn't give too much away.*
5 This book certainly *lived up to my expectations.*

5 Brainstorm the topic

Work with a partner and answer the questions. Note down the best ideas.

1 What kind of books did you like as a child?
2 Did you have a favourite? Was it an adventure story, a fantasy, a ghost story, some other type of book? Did it have illustrations? Did it have any memorable characters? Give a brief outline of the plot.
3 Would you recommend this book for other children to read? Why/Why not? Is there any other children's book that you would recommend more?
4 Which of the following do you feel to be important in a good children's book? Is anything else important?

- adventure
- fantasy
- humour
- imagination
- ingenuity
- suspense
- wit

6 Make a plan

Choose the best ideas you brainstormed and complete a paragraph plan for your review. (Use as many paragraphs as you need.)

Plan

Paragraph 1 / Introduction

Title of book, genre, general introduction to the book

Paragraph 2

....

Paragraph 3

....

Paragraph 4

....

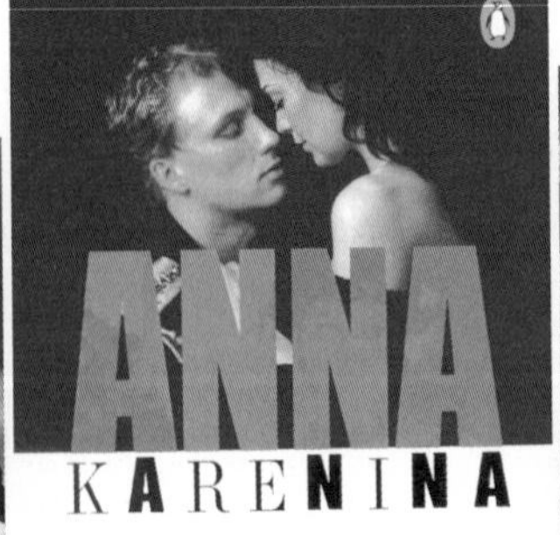

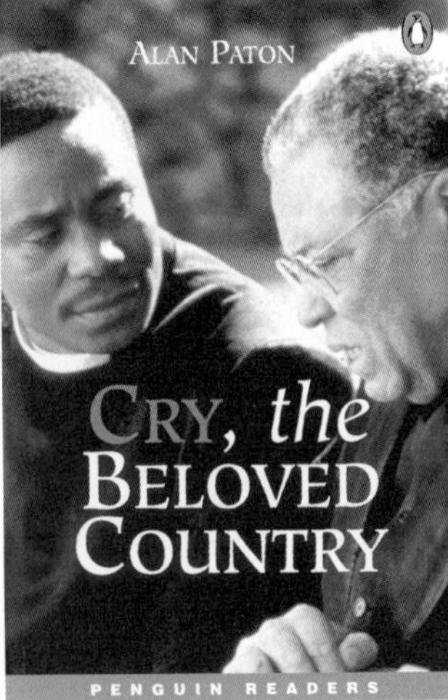

7 Compare two reviews

Imagine you are an examiner. Read the two reviews A and B below. Then go through this list and tick the appropriate column. You may tick both columns if necessary. Which review is a better answer to the exam question?

Which review:

		A	B
1	contains language that is natural and fluent?	☐	☐
2	has a good range of structures?	☐	☐
3	has a good range of expressions and collocations?	☐	☐
4	contains a good range of appropriate vocabulary?	☐	☐
5	contains language that is virtually error free?	☐	☐
6	is written in an appropriate register: neutral in tone but making the writer's feelings clear?	☐	☐
7	is well organised with good paragraphing?	☐	☐
8	has a clear introduction and conclusion?		
9	will leave the reader well informed about the book in question?	☐	☐
10	has answered the exam question in full?	☐	☐

Review A

Harry Potter and the Prisoner of Azkaban

Children have always loved books that challenge their imagination and appeal to their sense of humour. The success of the Harry Potter books is probably due to the fact that the author meets these two demands so successfully.

At the beginning of the book we meet the hero, Harry, who is a pupil at Hogwart's boarding school. The staff and pupils at the school are archetypal figures: the goody-goody student, the bully, the unfair teacher who always picks on certain students. What makes this school different is that it is a school for wizards and witches, and the everyday lives of all those at the school are permeated by magic.

The plot is gripping – a murderer has escaped from the prison of Azkaban and is at large in the school. He is being hunted by the Dementors, terrifying hooded figures that suck out the souls of their prey. Harry and his friends are forced to fight against the forces of darkness. Each chapter of the book ends in a cliff-hanger, which keeps the reader desperately turning the pages to see what happens next.

The characters are very well drawn and most readers can identify with them easily. Harry is the hero of the book but he is also sensitive and vulnerable. His best friends are Hermione and Ron; Hermione is the typical school swot but she is also loyal and resourceful; Ron is full of fun and mischief and sticks by his friends through thick and thin.

What lifts this book above others of its type and makes it an ideal read for children is the wit,

humour and sheer ingenuity with which it is written. The author has moved beyond the usual formula for children's books and come up with wildly inventive, funny scenes mixed with truly frightening. The story is totally convincing for children because she makes the world of Hogwart's School of Witchcraft and Wizardry as real as life at a normal school, but much more fantastic and exciting. If you are wondering what to give a young relative for a gift, look no further. Any child would be delighted to get a copy of this amazing book.

Review B

Pirate Diary

The Journal of Jake Carpenter

This illustrated book is a fabulous story that is also very witty.

It is the story of a boy who lives in Virginia in the eighteenth century. One day he went to sea in a boat and then was taken captive by a group of pirates. He spent weeks on the pirate ship and got to know all about their lives. The story is not actual fact. It didn't really happen. But the details in the book are very well researched and based on fact.

It's got lots of facts about sailing ships at that time and about the equipment they had and the customs of the sailors. It tells you a lot about why men became pirates (because they got fed up with being treated so badly on normal ships) and it's even got notes at the end that tell you more about the history of the time, so it's like having a history lesson but it makes it more enjoyable.

The story is written like a diary. Jake writes all his adventures in it. Some of the things that happen are quite bloodthirsty. There is rather a lot of blood in the pictures because the pirates cut bits off their victims and kill them. Some kids might not like this.

The illustrations are very good. They are very clear and colourful and humorous, but they are sometimes rather scary. Most young children enjoy pictures and adventure stories so I reckon they will enjoy this book very much.

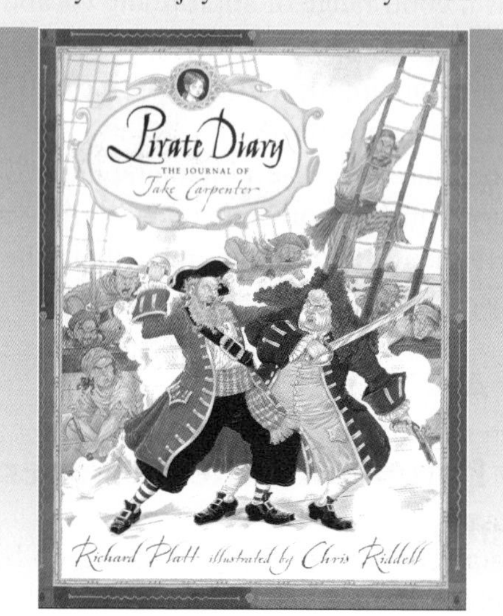

8 Think about language

Complete the sentences below with words and phrases from **Review A**.

1. The characters in the book are recognisable types. In fact, they are ....
2. Our History teacher is very unfair and always .... on me!
3. An atmosphere of joy and laughter .... the book, which partly accounts for its appeal.
4. In the first chapter, the police are looking for a dangerous criminal who is at .... in the city.
5. The pirates roam the seas looking for ships laden with treasure, which they hunt down like a wolf does its ....
6. *The Lord of the Rings* is a long story in which the peoples of Middle Earth battle against the .... of darkness.
7. The author ends all her chapters with a(n) ...., which means that you have to turn over the page to see what will happen next.
8. The characters are well .... and incredibly true to life.
9. The heroine of the book is a brave but .... young woman who manages to triumph over adversity.
10. One of the characters is a very clever student whom the others regard as a(n) ....
11. My best friend and I have always stood by each other through .... and thin.
12. I really admire the .... of the plot; it is one of the cleverest and most original I have read for a long time.

9 Think about tenses

Look back at **Review A**. Which tenses does the writer use to outline the plot in Paragraph 3? Underline examples.

10 Exam practice: Write a book review

You are going to write a book review. Read the exam question and follow the instructions below.

Part 2

Write your answer in **300–350 words** in an appropriate style.

A magazine you sometimes contribute to has a regular page entitled 'A Good Read'. The editor has invited you to write a review of a classic novel for this page and to explain its enduring popularity.

Write your **review**.

- **Brainstorm the topic**
  Note down a description of the book, including a brief outline of the plot and the main characters. Remember that it's much easier to write about a book you have actually read.
- **Make a plan**
  Make a paragraph plan, so that your review will be well organised. Make sure you write a clear introduction and conclusion.
- **Think about vocabulary**
  Try to use some of the words and expressions you have learnt in this unit.
- **Think about tenses**
  Use a range of present tenses, including the Present Perfect, to outline the plot.

20 Writing a review of a place

1 Read the question

Read the exam question below carefully.

Part 2

Write your answer in **300–350 words** in an appropriate style.

You write a regular column for your local newspaper. A new hotel has opened in your town and you were shown round it recently. While some features of the hotel impressed you, you thought that other areas left room for improvement. You have now been asked by the editor of your newspaper to write a review of the hotel.

Write your **review**.

exam information

In Part 2 of the exam, you may be asked to write a review of a hotel, a restaurant, or some other place.

2 Think about your reader

Work with a partner. Look at the exam question again and answer the following questions.

1 For what purpose are you writing? To evaluate something? To criticise something? For some other reason?
2 Are you writing your review for
   a a school magazine?
   b a newspaper?
   c some other publication?
3 Will your readers expect your review to be
   a neutral/formal?
   b very informal?

3 Identify the key points in the question

Work with a partner. Look at the exam question again and answer the following questions.

1 What have you been asked to write about?
2 How do you know about the place? When did it open?
3 Were you impressed by the place? Did you find aspects to criticise?

exam tip

There are *at least* two parts to most questions in Part 2 of the exam. To pass the exam, you must cover all the parts. Make sure you give each of them sufficient attention in your answer.